ADVANCE PRAISE FOR *SPIRITUAL SOBRIETY*

"*SPIRITUAL SOBRIETY* OFFERS A PROVOCATIVE AND INSIGHTFUL COUNTERBAL-ance to the indulgent emotionalism that characterizes much of modern-day religious experience. Drawing from experts and everyday people as well as her own story of religious addiction, Elizabeth Esther points helpfully toward the line between *holding* religious beliefs and *using* them. *Spiritual Sobriety* isn't just for religion addicts. It's for everyone."

—Karen Swallow Prior, Ph.D., author of
Booked: Literature in the Soul of Me and
*Fierce Convictions—The Extraordinary Life of
Hannah More: Poet, Reformer, Abolitionist*

"WITH THE SKILL OF A SEASONED TEACHER AND THE CARE OF A DEAR FRIEND, Elizabeth Esther lights the path forward for those escaping unhealthy re-ligious environments and habits. Rarely is a single book this personal and practical, compelling and profound. With *Spiritual Sobriety,* Esther estab-lishes herself as one of our culture's most important healers. Her words of hope and healing will undoubtedly impact generations."

—Rachel Held Evans, bestselling author of
Searching for Sunday and *A Year of Biblical Womanhood*

"NO MATTER YOUR RELIGIOUS ADDICTIONS OR THEOLOGICAL POSITIONS, OR how you plan to vote in the next election, *the compassionate kindness of God cannot be moved.* With an unexpected blend of tender vulnerability and cutting honesty, Elizabeth Esther emerges from a spiritually abusive past as a woman who takes that truth to heart, learning to be kind to her-self in the process. Her willingness to stay small in the presence of God is perhaps what I admire most about her."

—Emily P. Freeman, author of *Simply Tuesday*

"IN *SPIRITUAL SOBRIETY*, ELIZABETH ESTHER ASKS THIS INSIGHTFULLY SCAN-dalous question—are we mainlining religion, using it as an anesthetizing agent against the pains and questions of life? With the incisive style that has become her hallmark, Esther draws us from the narcotic numbing of so much religion, and invites us to imagine a vibrant faith of loving and sober connection with God."

—Seth Haines, author of *Coming Clean*

"*SPIRITUAL SOBRIETY* IS AN IMPORTANT BOOK. IT'S IMPORTANT BECAUSE SOME folks, like myself, have survived harmful spiritual experiences and have been left to untangle the effects of spiritual addiction. And it's important because other folks, regardless of their experiences, are unaware of what spiritual wholeness—sobriety—even looks like. With her characteristic honesty, intelligence, and wisdom, Elizabeth Esther shines a light on top-ics that prefer to hide in darkness—and illuminates the way to freedom. Read, and then share, this book."

—Zach J. Hoag, author of *After the Apocalypse*

"ELIZABETH HAS BEEN THROUGH DARKNESS THAT COULD HAVE STOPPED HER in her tracks, but she presses on, bringing good news to those of us who need to hear it most. She dismantles all the ways we become codependent on unhealthy religious systems while also offering us a fresh hope in the God who transcends those systems. *Spiritual Sobriety* is not merely a good book—it is a crucial book. A game changer in the conversation about faith and God."

—Rob Carmack, pastor of Collective Church in Roanoke, Texas

ALSO BY ELIZABETH ESTHER

*Girl at the End of the World: My Escape from Fundamentalism
in Search of Faith with a Future*

Spiritual Sobriety

Stumbling Back to Faith
When Good Religion Goes Bad

ELIZABETH ESTHER

CONVERGENT
BOOKS
NEW YORK

Published in the United States by Convergent Books, an imprint of the Crown
Publishing Group, a division of Penguin Random House LLC, New York.
www.crownpublishing.com

CONVERGENT BOOKS is a registered trademark and
its open book colophon is a trademark
of Penguin Random House LLC.

Library of Congress Cataloging-in-Publication Data
is available upon request.

ISBN 978-0-307-73189-0
eBook ISBN 978-0-307-73190-6

Printed in the United States of America

Book design: Helene Berinsky
Cover design: Jessie Bright
Cover background image: SchmitzOlaf

10 9 8 7 6 5 4 3 2 1

First Edition

FOR MY CHILDREN

Jewel, James, Jude, Jorai & Jasiel

CONTENTS

Spiritual Sobriety

1

When Good Faith Goes Bad

Spiritual Sobriety Defined

For some "faithful"—and for unbelievers, too—"faith" seems to be a kind of drunkenness, an anesthetic, that keeps [them] from realizing and believing that anything can ever go wrong.

—*THOMAS MERTON*

THE FIRST TIME I GOT HIGH ON GOD I WAS FIVE YEARS OLD.

I'd heard that accepting Jesus as my personal Lord and Savior would make me happy and also win me a spot in heaven, where I would live forever with my family and all the other people who didn't watch R-rated movies. So, I knelt on the floor of our rental home, bowed my head over clasped hands, and asked Jesus to come live in my heart.

And lo, the heavens opened and amazing grace, how sweet the sound, made a wretch like me high for one whole day. All my little-girl worries and fears were whisked away as if by magic. I sang, I danced—scratch that, I couldn't dance because dancing led straight to fornication—*but still*. There was singing! There was preaching! There was scrambling atop the kitchen table and leading my stuffed animals in a rousing chorus of "What can wash away my sins? Nothing but the blood of Jesus!"

The next day I asked Jesus into my heart again. Of course

I did. Who wouldn't want another taste of sparkling, bubbly glory?

So, I clasped my hands the same way. I bowed my head the same way. I said the same prayer—but it didn't work the same way. I wasn't rocketed to the heights. There was no surge of zeal, no burst of God-infused energy. *Huh*, I thought. *Maybe I need to pray harder.*

Clasp hands. Bow head. Pray words. Really *mean* it.

Wait.

Wait.

Please hurry up, God. I need to feel the feeling.

Nothing.

Okay, well, I'll ask Jesus into my heart again tomorrow . . .

I tell this little story about myself for two reasons. In a kinda cute, five-year-old way, it reveals the promise at the heart of Christian belief—with God, a newer, better life is possible. It also reveals how beliefs and behaviors, even in such a young person, can begin to show distortions. For me, those distortions went on to do great harm. They pushed me away from healthy relationships and healthy thinking.

They pushed me away from God.

How surprising that what has the potential to make us better can become the very thing that makes us sick! How can something so good and innocent morph into unhealthy beliefs, feelings, and habits?

The Misuse of God

Growing up in a highly religious family, I discovered plenty of opportunities for indulging my God-habit: I knew my Bible so well that when I raced other kids to find obscure Scripture references, I got there first; I could proclaim a gospel message in sixty seconds or less; I wrote essays on theology to win my minister-dad's approval; I was so "on fire for God" that I wasn't ashamed to preach on street corners; I sang hymns with my eyes closed like a truly spiritual Christian; I said "Amen!" and took copious notes during my grandfather's teaching; I hated my "sinful flesh" more than other people hated theirs; and I regularly surrendered all to Jesus—preferably in front of a big crowd.

I didn't know it at the time, of course, but I was creating a pattern of behavior that closely mirrored alcoholism or addiction—except I wasn't consuming drugs to alter my moods, I was consuming God. I didn't have access to chemical substances—we were intensely devout, conservative Christians—so I used what was available: religious beliefs. I habitually "used" God and all things church to numb pain and feel good. Even when my substance of choice stopped working, I couldn't stop.

As with any other addiction, my overzealous religious practice came with a dark side. There was the uncomfortable, sometimes painful letdown once the spiritual high wore off, followed by the ache of withdrawal and, eventually, a renewed craving that drove me to search for my next fix.

For me, religion was all—or mostly—about how it made me feel. I wanted to feel close to God, cherished, chosen, *special*. Maybe you can relate. For many of us, religion also offers a sense of being in control; it becomes a way (we think) to get God to do what we want. A woman once shared with me that she deferred to God "as if my ever-more-complete submission would force God's hand into blessing me with abundance, like financial success, a devoted partner, and cheerful, obedient children."[1]

In my opinion, this transactional use of God—I pay God with surrender, zeal, or commitment so that God will repay me with good feelings or other blessings—has more to do with idolatry than with authentic Christianity. And experts say this is a common characteristic of treating religion like a drug.

Does spiritualized trading sound familiar to you? It does to me.

Hi, I'm Elizabeth and I'm a religious addict.

Addicted to *What*?

Perhaps that word *addict* stops you. How can someone be addicted to God? How could a passionate spirituality ever be negative or harmful? You might even be worried that I'm some kind of undercover atheist trying to pry you away from a faith and a God you hold dear.

Please hear me: I'm not to trying to argue against God. I'm not disrespecting church or any religious person or creed. Not at all. I'm speaking as a follower of Jesus who cherishes some hard-won understandings that have made a better life possible for me and countless others.

I'll admit, when I first heard the term *religious addiction*, I thought it was too dramatic to describe my experience.

1. Sandra. "Survey Questionnaire for Spiritual Sobriety." E-mail interview by author. April 25, 2015.

But addiction comes down to a simple distinction: For balanced individuals, the cost of the hangovers or other negative outcomes becomes a sufficient reason to reexamine their thinking and change behavior. An addict, on the other hand, repeatedly engages in the same behavior, regardless of the negative consequences.

Christian authors have further defined religious addiction as "the state of being dependent on a spiritually mood-altering system,"[2] concluding that religious addicts "might as well take a drink, swallow a pill, or inject a drug. The intent is not to worship God but to alter their perception of reality. They are religious junkies, obsessed with mood alteration and a quick fix to face life."[3]

These definitions sound harsh, but stay with me, because the cost of our addiction is harsh, too. Pastor and spiritual director Kathy Escobar describes how this dependency often starts:

> Many men and women have an unaddressed addiction to church services or spiritual experiences where they feel wowed. We get hooked on amazing music, powerful preaching, and the hour-long Sunday experience. We come to church seeking a spiritual high that will help us make it through the upcoming week. . . . Instead of addressing the realities of what we're really thinking, feel-

---

2. David Johnson and Jeffrey VanVonderen, *The Subtle Power of Spiritual Abuse* (Minneapolis, MN: Bethany House Publishers, 1991), 190.

3. Stephen Arterburn and Jack Felton, *Toxic Faith: Experiencing Healing from Painful Spiritual Abuse* (Colorado Springs, CO: Shaw, 2001), 30.

ing, and experiencing in the dark places of our souls, we sometimes look for a quick, temporary fix instead.[4]

Therapists Stephen Arterburn and Jack Felton show what often happens next, describing the subtle yet devastating shifts that begin to hollow out our spiritual lives:

> [The religious addict has] embraced a counterfeit religion. God is not honored, and the relationship with him is not furthered. . . . Rather than retreat to the loving arms of God, they literally bury themselves in their compulsive acts. . . . The religious addict begins a gradual transition away from God. Church attendance is no longer based on the need to know God; the addict attends church to feel significant and secure. Prayers are no longer ways of communicating with God; the addict prays to have an experience as a person of God and takes pride in being able to talk of the hours spent in prayer.[5]

These people might sound whacko, but truth is, the addictive impulse is a human thing. On my blog I hear from so many decent people with good hearts who, without really knowing what was happening, got twisted up in something false and spiritually bruising.

The signs that something is wrong can pop up in the smallest ways.

---

4. Kathy Escobar, *Faith Shift: Finding Your Way Forward When Everything You Believe Is Coming Apart* (New York: Convergent Books, 2014), 56–57.

5. Arterburn and Felton, *Toxic Faith*, 98, 113.

Views from the Pews

Meet Joyce, a former fundamentalist, who had a moment of clarity when her husband announced that, after twenty-two years of marriage, he wanted a divorce. "I was sitting on our boat, tension hanging heavily," she wrote, "and I thought, *If only I had my Bible I would be okay.* I realized that sounded an awful lot like 'If only I had a drink.' That was when I started exploring fundamentalism as an addiction."[6]

James wrote to compare his experience as an alcoholic with his experiences with religion:

> With alcohol, I felt like I *had* to have it. With religious practice, I felt like I *ought* to have it. I was addicted to the pressure to feel fulfilled (although I never was). I used music as an escape from intense religious shame and anxiety. [The religious practice] was very pagan: instead of "If you sacrifice a goat, it will rain," we had "If you tithe, you'll have financial success" or "If you avoid public school, your children won't be tainted."[7]

The fixation can extend even to practical matters, such as planning for retirement. Kelly grew up in a household of family members so obsessed with the end of the world that they signed up for a high-level "sponsorship" with an end-times prophecy organization rather than start a 401(k) or make

6. "Fundamentalism as an Addiction." E-mail interview by author. April 14, 2015.

7. "Survey Questionnaire for Spiritual Sobriety." E-mail interview by author. April 25, 2015.

other financial arrangements. "They were convinced they'd be raptured long before retirement savings would be necessary," she explained.[8]

Brenda explained to me how summers spent at a church camp created emotional confusion for her:

> I went to Bible camp every summer for ten years straight. Every time I would ride the emotional high of worship and intense preaching/teaching. I thrived on the emotional connection I felt to God, but it always dissipated as soon as I got back to my regularly scheduled life.
>
> As an adult, I still [felt] vulnerable to emotional worship services. I'd go week after week, desperate to feel an emotional connection to God. When the preacher closed out the night by saying how amazing it had been to experience God's presence, I'd go out to my car and sob because I didn't feel any connection at all.[9]

There's nothing quite like having our hopes for overnight transformation dashed against the rocks of reality to slap us awake from our religious stupor. When we come down from the high, we tend to wake up with a hangover of sorts: a guilty sting resulting from wasted time, wasted money, and wasted emotional energy. This letdown is an important indicator

---

8. "Survey Questionnaire for Spiritual Sobriety." E-mail interview by author. April 25, 2015.

9. "Survey Questionnaire for Spiritual Sobriety." E-mail interview by author. April 25, 2015.

that something is wrong. If we behaved in healthier ways, we wouldn't feel the gnawing despair of having spent ourselves on a mirage.

But we don't have to stay stuck. With humility, an open spirit, and courage, we can escape the maze and find our way home.

The issue is this: an obsession with spiritual beliefs, rituals, and pursuits that initially helps us but eventually removes our power to make healthy decisions and brings significant harm to us and to those close to us.

The answer: spiritual sobriety.

A Way to Live at Peace with God and the World

Spiritual sobriety asks us to examine the ways we've treated religion like a drug and to replace those behaviors with healthier expressions of spirituality. It's finding a way to nurture ourselves and be of service to others—even while our questions remain unanswered.

My purpose in writing this book is to show you a path out of harmful behavior and toward a healthier spirituality that empowers you to live at peace with God and the world around you. My description of that path is learning spiritual sobriety. I define the term like this:

Spiritual sobriety is a serene, moderate way of living in which people abstain from treating God, religion, or a belief system like a drug; refrain from using religion as a punishment against others or ourselves; seek to be rigorously honest rather than unfailingly good;[10] and retain the best of their spiritual devotion in positive, life-enhancing ways.

I've spent many hours contemplating—and seeking to live into—these words. I encourage you to do the same. Begin by reading the sentence through a few times, pausing as you go. Let its promises—stated and implied—speak to you of new possibilities. Then turn each part into a picture of your new spiritual life:

- "Spiritual sobriety is my serene and moderate way of life."
- "I abstain from treating God, religion, or beliefs like a drug."
- "I refrain from using religion as punishment against anyone."
- "Instead, I seek to be rigorously honest—not unfailingly good."
- "And I retain the best of spiritual devotion in positive, life-enhancing ways."

I hope that in these simple, sane statements you are seeing a hopeful and healing way forward. As you'll learn in the pages ahead, we don't have to reject our past. We don't have to dump God or our faith (although we might need distance for a while). We don't have to dump family and friends (even if we do need to set boundaries). Instead, we can learn to embrace our stories and become enriched by them.

---

10. The Augustine Fellowship, Sex and Love Addicts Anonymous, Fellowship-Wide Services, Inc., *Sex and Love Addicts Anonymous* (Boston: The Augustine Fellowship, Sex and Love Addicts Anonymous, Fellowship-Wide Services, Inc., first ed., 1986), 109.

My faith survived an apocalyptic childhood cult (more on that in chapter 2 and in my first book, *Girl at the End of the World*). Whatever your story, I suspect your questions, hurts, or despair surrounding God, church, and religion are just as challenging and overwhelming to you as mine were to me. But no matter how sick or unsure or afraid you feel, I assure you that recovery and healing *are* possible.

Once I realized that I was hooked on something (or in this case, a version of something) that was hurting me and others, I was motivated to change. The first step in recovery is always facing up to the desperate nature of our reality, then reaching out for help.

If you're still with me, I believe you've already taken that step.

Now that you've glimpsed the way forward, I invite you to take a deeper look at a very puzzling question. How did we go from happy, well-adjusted believers to not-so-happy believers in need of sobriety?

How Did We Get Here, and What Is Here Called?

This place where we find ourselves right now—on this page, in this unexpected life? You and I are not to blame. It's so important to just say it! We didn't make a conscious choice to treat religion this way. At whatever age we veered off track, we were just doing the best we could.

Our parents or other religious authority figures—in most cases, they were doing the best they could, too. Still, they took us into the theological and emotional weeds, often with really negative (and sometimes straight-on crazy) consequences.

What they presented to us as good and "holy" were actually very unhealthy behaviors—acting out of fear, paranoia, or judgment instead of love; obsessing and repressing when it came to sex; training us to strive ever harder to deserve what God had already given.

How were we supposed to know there were healthy ways of approaching God when the people we admired taught us that living intentionally with God looked like anything but freedom?

Again, we never meant to use God as a drug; we were just trying to make ourselves feel okay. We never meant to become so self-absorbed and dependent; we were just trying to survive this frustrating, unpredictable, painful, impossible thing called *life*. For the most part, we were just trying to be good Christians—rejoicing always! full of the peace that passeth understanding! glorying in our afflictions! counting not the cost!—but somehow, trying to be a good Christian ended up hurting us.

Researchers define our particular condition as a "process addiction," meaning it's about behaviors, not substances. It involves "any compulsive-like behavior that interferes with normal living and causes significant negative consequences in the person's family, work and social life."[11]

I'm not the first person to notice the similarities between experiencing religion and, say, gambling as mood elevators. As early as 1991, counselors and pastors were producing

---

11. Angie D. Wilson and Pennie Johnson, "Counselors' Understanding of Process Addiction: A Blind Spot in the Counseling Field." *The Professional Counselor*, October 2014. http://tpcjournal.nbcc.org/counselors-understanding-of-process-addiction-a-blind-spot-in-the-counseling-field/.

literature about the dangers of "toxic faith."[12] Father Leo Booth, an Episcopal priest specializing in recovery treatment programs, brought religious addiction to light in his pioneering book, *When God Becomes a Drug*. Booth defined it as "using God, a church, or a belief system as an escape from reality, in an attempt to find or elevate a sense of self-worth or well-being. It is using God or religion as a fix . . . as a weapon against ourselves or others."[13]

Religious studies professor Dr. Robert Minor explains, "A process becomes an addiction when the process becomes the center of life, the most important reason for living, when a person becomes dependent upon the process for mood-altering relief."[14] It's not that relief itself is a problem, but our dependence on it is. For religious addicts, this dependency might look like compulsively quoting Scripture to a friend in distress (or ourselves) rather than acknowledging uncomfortable emotions like anger, doubt, or sadness. Rather than facing reality and taking healthy actions, we addicts turn toward religious processes and rituals to relieve our painful feelings.

For example, in the cult atmosphere in which I grew up, doing the laundry wasn't tedious when it meant I was part of "God's amazing work in our generation" (especially if it was the preacher's laundry!). Mundane chores were transformed into twenty-four-karat God-plated riches that were being

---

12. Arterburn and Felton, *Toxic Faith*.

13. Leo Booth, *When God Becomes a Drug: Breaking the Chains of Religious Addiction and Abuse* (Los Angeles: J. P. Tarcher, 1991), 38.

14. Robert Neil Minor, PhD, *When Religion Is an Addiction* (St. Louis, MO: Humanity Works!, 2007), 34.

stored up in heaven for me. Everything *means* something, especially if that thing includes giving away your money.

My journey toward spiritual sobriety began when I realized I had a problem with the way I related to God. My problem was not owned by God, or my church, or my pastor. And blame was not helpful. The problem was *mine*—which meant I could do something about it.

From there, I began to see that my future did not need to be an extension of my past or even my present. I had choices. I could change. I could choose to live spiritually clean and sober.

What Sobriety Looks Like

Now that we have a clearer idea of the beast of addiction, let's illustrate more fully what the beauty of spiritual sobriety looks like.

COMMON BELIEFS AND BEHAVIORS OF SOBER CHRISTIANS

- We celebrate God's unconditional love for us and learn to trust again. We develop a daily relationship with God and do not fill our "God-need" with other people, places, or things. (More on this in chapter 3.)
- We replace religious superstition—*If I don't attend every service, God will punish me*—with common sense and practice self-care through proper nutrition, education, personal hygiene, and medical attention.
- We do not abuse, mistreat, or neglect our children for the sake of religion.

- We take responsibility for our behaviors and no longer blame other people, supernatural forces, or institutions for our own decisions and actions.
- We do not presume to speak for God, preferring rather to find common ground, respect the experiences of others, and build unity. We challenge ourselves to appreciate other expressions of spirituality and refrain from imposing our way of doing things. We do not offer unsolicited advice.
- Our behavior is moderate and intentional, free from compulsion, obsession, and extremism.
- We learn how to identify and express our true feelings. We replace self-loathing and perfectionism with love, acceptance, and compassion for ourselves.
- We recognize theological arguments as futile and use kind speech and civil behavior when expressing our beliefs. We do not insist on being right.
- We give generously and cheerfully without the ulterior motives of "buying" our way into heaven or earning God's favor.
- We prioritize our commitments to children and family above our commitments to a religious leader or organization. We avoid situations that may compromise our spiritual, physical, emotional, or psychological well-being.
- We offer the gift of our presence in the present, allowing God to take care of our afterlife.

If this profile sounds too idealistic for you, be encouraged. It describes where we want to go, who we want to be, not necessarily where we are at any given moment. As with all forms of sobriety, the journey to spiritual sobriety will take work. There is no magic formula that produces immediate results. But our way of life is real, and doable, as thousands of flourishing people of faith before us can attest.

The main promise of religion is not, after all, that we always feel better *right now* (although that is often a happy by-product). Rather, authentic religion reminds us that we are part of something much larger and ultimately more fulfilling than our own personal narrative. The point is to become so free from our own, limiting behaviors that we are readily able to love and serve others.

In the pages ahead, I'll share with you my own journey toward spiritual and emotional health. As you'll see, it has been a bumpy road that included a stint in rehab and required a total overhaul of my relationship with God. I'll show you what it means to develop a spiritually sober thought life and how this new way of thinking can guide our words and actions. I'll also lay out a road map for integrating spiritual sobriety in our relationships and churches. Each chapter comes with an interactive element to help you process and integrate what you've read in a more personal way.

And don't miss the small group conversation guide at the end of the book. Together, we'll walk a path that is, as my friend Jane says, "Sloowwwwwbriety." The going might be slow, but it's also how dysfunction gets gradually erased and imperfection becomes the source of our most surprising strength.

Practice Your Spiritual Sobriety

In this section, which also appears in the next few chapters, you will find a prayer, an encouraging Scripture, and several journaling questions to help you more deeply reflect on what spiritual sobriety means for you. It's advantageous to meet with friends and share these discoveries; spiritual sobriety is best served when it is practiced within a safe, affirming community of like-minded friends. Of course, feel free to work on these questions alone; many of us have been wounded in religious communities and need time to process our recovery in healing solitude. Whether you choose to practice your spiritual sobriety alone or in a group, I hope you will find this recovery work as healing as I have.

Prayer:

God, give me the courage to examine the ways I've used religion like a drug. Free me from my addictive behaviors and show me the path toward spiritual sobriety.

Promise:

"So then, let us not be like others, who are asleep, but let us be awake and sober . . . since we belong to the day, let us be sober, putting on faith and love as a breastplate, and the hope of salvation as a helmet." 1 Thessalonians 5:6 & 8, NIV

Journaling/Group Questions:

- Father Leo Booth describes religious addiction as "using God, a church, or a belief system as an escape from reality. . . . It is using God as a fix." Describe some ways you've used God as a means to an end—i.e., "if I do *x*, God will do *y*." Why is this transactional approach to God unhealthy?

- Have you ever hoped for spiritual transformation only to wake up the next morning and discover things are exactly as they were? That nothing has changed? How did this make you feel? How did this negatively impact your relationship with God?

- Dr. Robert Minor says a process becomes an addiction when "a person becomes dependent on the process for mood-altering relief." Examine your attachment to religious processes or rituals: Do you feel like you can't live without them? Do you feel a constant need to "amp up" your faith? Do you feel worried that your supply of God-feelings might run out? Pause for a moment to look at the motivation behind your strong attachment to religious processes. Is there fear? Insecurity? Scarcity?

- Spiritual sobriety is the calm, thoughtful, moderate practice of spiritual or religious beliefs. It is not excessive, compulsive, or addictive. Can you think of someone you know (or admire) who embodies these qualities? How would you describe them in three words? Write it down.

- When we start a journey of recovery, it helps to imagine the destination or the kind of person we want to become. The person you described above can be a role model for your spiritual sobriety. You can make their qualities your own by setting specific intentions (or goals). Write down three goals you want to work toward in your spiritual sobriety.

You are here now. You are awake now.
Welcome to Spiritual Sobriety.

2

Twisted Belief

Reality and the Religious Addict

I am terrified by this dark thing
That sleeps in me;
All day I feel its soft, feathery turnings, its malignity.

—SYLVIA PLATH, "ELM"

WHEN YOU GROW UP BELIEVING JESUS IS IN CHARGE OF stoplights, it's pretty much a foregone conclusion that you will have distorted thoughts and feelings in other ways, too.

I was raised in a fundamentalist Christian cult. We were born-again believers convinced that the end of the world was imminent. We didn't buy homes, invest in retirement savings, watch TV, listen to secular music, or use credit cards. Everything in our lives was about preaching the gospel before Jesus returned. Everything we did was weighted with vast eternal significance. Even sitting at a stoplight had spiritual implications.

A red light was never just a red light.

People in my childhood church were always telling stories about how a red light prevented them from getting involved in a car accident that was happening farther down the road. Or how they had asked God to save them a parking space at the mall, and praise the Lord, he totally did. Unfortunately, a childhood spent in an environment like this really messed with my understanding of God. Imagine my surprise when I asked God for legitimate things ("Please make old Brother C. stop asking for long hugs") and God didn't follow through.

And that wasn't the least of it. As a child, I was spanked heavily and frequently. I grew up believing I was a vile, wicked sinner deserving nothing but God's wrath. My only hope was to cleanse myself from all wickedness before the world ended in 1988—yes, that was the date my preacher-grandfather believed Jesus was returning to earth.

Adding ballast to my obsessive thoughts about sinfulness, the end of the world, and wondering what the next stoplight would portend were emotionally charged church services, Bible studies, fellowship gatherings, and familial relationships. It seemed as though maintaining a supreme level of expectation, gratitude, and submission kept the flock wired for the second coming. It also cemented painful platitudes and chronic disappointment—in myself and others—in my personality.

Spoiler alert: The world didn't end in 1988, which meant I didn't get raptured into the cotton-candy clouds but had to finish growing up among a bunch of fellow religious addicts. Which meant some distorted emotional journeys and confusing thought processes.

The Big Show

As I've described, part of my experience as a child was histrionic emotionalism connected with spiritual matters. Maybe like me you've experienced the euphoria—and desolation—of religious services aimed at drawing in the faithful via lights, sound, and deep feeling.

Many religious events are intentionally designed to deliver intense emotional experiences. There's the ubiquitous mood lighting so that you can see only what is meant to be seen—i.e., the stage and the pretty people standing on it. Loud music ensures you hear only what is meant to be heard—i.e., not your own thoughts. Several high-energy warm-up acts make you feel only what you're supposed to feel—i.e., excited about what's going to happen. And all around you are hundreds of people who are seeing, hearing, and feeling the same thing. By the time the featured attraction steps on stage—whether that's the preacher, Oprah, or a worship band—you're so amped up you'll hand over your body, soul, and wallet.

It doesn't even occur to you that this might be destructive, because feeling elated is the desired outcome.

Sandra remembers believing that if she just tried harder, she would feel a comforting closeness to God; then she recognized who was pulling the strings.

While I experienced "feeling God's presence in a mighty way" during worship services, I usually assumed it was my fault that the feeling didn't last through the week. If I were a better Christian, prayed more earnestly, read the Bible more diligently, renounced my willfulness more thoroughly, then I would "feel God" all the time.

It wasn't until I attended [several missionary conferences in a row] over the course of one summer that the falsity of emotional frenzy became apparent. This wasn't God's presence "working mightily among us." This was nothing more than the emotional overload of guilt and ecstasy compounded by lack of sleep, travel fatigue, and too much coffee.[1]

Laura recalls the vigorous experiences of Christian conferences and their damaging aftermath: "I had to stop attending women's conferences because it induced some kind of artificial high that translated to depression once I came down off that 'mountain-top experience.'"[2]

Brenda experienced intense religious thoughts and feelings even as a child. In the programs she attended annually, she encountered the high—but soon after, the low. "We were given advice on how to keep the 'fire' going, but no one ever questioned the whole format of the experience in the first place. . . . Emotional manipulation seemed to be the entire point of gatherings like that."

The letdown after religious intoxication is often brutal. RAs (religious addicts) wonder what happened, what they did "wrong," how they had offended the God they wanted so much to appease. Despair often follows as the RA keeps reaching for the holiness and happiness he or she craves.

When taking first steps toward spiritual sobriety, reality is a wall you'll have to hit. Believe it or not, reality is a good thing.

1. "Survey Questionnaire for Spiritual Sobriety." E-mail interview by author. April 25, 2015.

2. "Survey Questionnaire for Spiritual Sobriety." E-mail interview by author. April 25, 2015.

Where Sobriety Begins

After I left the cult at age twenty-five, I had a lot of work to do, not the least of which was learning to deal with reality. Life on the outside wasn't what I expected. Everything seemed random. There were no standardized belief systems; people believed whatever they wanted, and they didn't behave the way I thought they would. They were so very people-ish; everyone had feelings, everyone had opinions, everyone had his or her own interests, hobbies, concerns, ideas, and ways of doing things. What did I have? I had a whole set of outdated rules and antiquated ways of living that didn't apply to this fast-moving world. I faced some very real new feelings.

I felt disconnected. Estranged. Like I didn't fit in. Which seemed just as uncomfortable as addiction!

I soon learned that many people feel this way, even if they don't talk about it. Loneliness, anxiety, and uncertainty are the de facto realities of life in post-9/11 America. The automatic garage door goes up at the beginning of the day and down when you come home. Maybe you see the person who lives in the house next to yours, maybe you don't. And weakness—or even the appearance of weakness—is to be avoided at all costs.

"So, what do you do?" is the question I hear most often from RAs. Apparently, activity is what identifies people, makes them happy and successful. But all this doing doesn't mitigate the inexplicable parts of reality. It doesn't resolve the fact that things don't go according to plan, that good, smart people can become obsessed with God, and even though we do everything in our power to achieve holiness, we often feel empty and sad. Despite attaining productivity in our careers or satisfaction in our family lives, we still have this gnawing ache inside us.

The religious addict in me doesn't like this reality, because it doesn't line up with my neat little beliefs about how the world works. One inexplicable reality that I never wanted to admit was my lifelong struggle with depression. I always thought—and was always told—that my chronic "sadness" (we didn't even call it *depression*) was the result of weak faith. Depression was *my* fault. If I just prayed more, read my Bible more consistently, repented more often, I'd be cured.

I learned the hard way that a big part of my spiritual sobriety meant being honest about everything, including my physical and mental health. The more I lived in denial and pretended that my depression wasn't real or that it was just a temporary interruption, the more suffering I experienced.

A few years ago, a significant depressive episode reminded me yet again that living in reality is vital to my recovery from religious addiction.

I stared at my psychiatrist through puffy eyes. He was very matter-of-fact, rapidly flipping through my chart as if he'd seen all this before. I envied his certitude, his sense of calm, the orderly assurance of his polished, tasseled loafers. I twisted the tissue in my hand and told myself I wasn't the only frazzled, burned-out mom who emptied his Kleenex box. I regretted my raggedy yoga pants.

"This is your . . . third depressive episode?" he asked, squinting at some writing on my chart.

"Something like that." This latest episode felt like a rogue black wave, rising up out of the sea and blindsiding me as I walked along the shore of my life. It sucked me into the dark depths. I tumbled around not knowing which way was up or down, holding my breath. Other times, depression had lowered over me like a glass box. I watched my life unfold before me as if I were standing behind a feelings-proof, one-sided mirror. I could see my life happening, but I couldn't feel it. I couldn't engage it.

"And why did you go off your medication?"

His tone was curious, not judgmental. Still, I felt judged. *They're all out to get me! It's a conspiracy.* I bit a fingernail.

"Well?" he prompted.

"Um. I thought I was cured?"

He raised a curious-not-judgmental eyebrow.

I felt the need to elaborate—as if rational explanations were something my broken-down brain was capable of right then. "I was feeling so much better! I thought I didn't need medication anymore! I mean, I just get blue sometimes. Who doesn't cry a little bit every day?"

He cleared his throat, smiled, and crossed one leg. The tassels on his loafers glinted softly in the warm light of his desk lamp. "I see."

He scribbled something very important in my chart. "Elizabeth, you were feeling better *because* you were on medication."

Ugh.

"If this is your third depressive episode, the likelihood of your having another episode in your lifetime is quite high. Why take that chance?"

I blurted an answer before I could stop myself. "Because I don't want to be one of those crazy people who needs to be on medication to function!"

"First of all, you're not crazy. You're depressed. And second, if you were nearsighted, would you be upset about having to wear glasses every day?"

"Yes, I would."

I was being difficult, as my mother might say. But my doctor seemed unfazed. He chuckled a bit as he wrote me a prescription.

"But you'd still wear those glasses, wouldn't you?" He handed me the crisp rectangle of paper.

"I guess so."

"Do you want to feel better?"

"Yes," I said. And that was true.

"Then take this medication every day, and come see me in two weeks."

"Am I going to be on antidepressants for the rest of my life?" I asked.

He met my gaze evenly. "I'd recommend that, yes."

His words were the blast of a trumpet, and like the walls of Jericho, my ego fell down.

This is the moment I look back on and define as the day when I finally admitted I had a problem and needed help. It was an early step toward sobriety.

It was the moment when I met *misericordia*.

Merciful Lovingkindness

In medieval times when a knight was mortally wounded in combat, another knight would use a long, thin dagger called a *misericord* to deliver the mercy stroke and end his suffering. This deathblow was considered an act of compassion.

Misericordia is derived from the Latin words for "merciful" and "heart."[3] Essentially, *misericordia* means a humane kindness that springs from the heart.

The prophet Isaiah wrote, "It was our sicknesses He carried; it was our diseases that weighed him down."[4] The *misericordia* of God, then, is God suffering *with* us. This is not a distant, angry god waiting to judge us. This is the God who is intimately acquainted with our grief. This is the God who is "gracious and full of compassion, slow to anger and great in mercy."[5]

So often we're convinced—due to what we learned as RAs—that God is out to get us, that he's watching our every move, ready to judge and condemn us when we screw up. It's hard to ask a god like that for help. He's too scary! And anyway, why would God want to help religious addicts like us when we've compulsively misused him?

This is why the concept of *misericordia* gives me hope. It suggests something about the compassion of God that I rarely experienced in my addiction. It means that no matter

---

3. "Etymology of the Latin Word 'misericordia,'" MyEtymology.com. Accessed May 20, 2015. http://www.myetymology.com/latin/misericordia.html.

4. Isaiah 53:4 NLT (New Living Translation).

5. Psalm 145:8 NKJV (New King James Verion).

how many times I fail, God's mercy and lovingkindness are never exhausted.

In the New Testament, St. Paul said, "I want to do what is good, but I don't. I don't want to do what is wrong, but I do it anyway."[6] Isn't this the very essence of addiction? We try to do the right thing but urgently do the things we don't want to do. We try and we fail, and then we try and fail again.

Oh, wretched addict that I am! Who will deliver me from this body of death?

The language of this passage in Romans 7 is so fraught. St. Paul even goes so far as to say that he isn't the one doing the wrong thing; it's the power of sin within him that does it. That's pretty compelling—the idea that what drives us to behave addictively is not our true selves but rather a different power, a sick self living inside us.

This is why calling addiction a disease makes sense to me. Addicts don't want to do what they do. But they can't stop without help. Their sick selves have taken the wheel, and their true selves are hanging on for dear life in the backseat. When the addiction is behind the wheel, it's easy to forget that the true self even exists. We may begin to think that's all we are: crazy, sick addicts who don't know how to stop ourselves from driving off a cliff.

Maybe we identify so closely with our sick selves that we don't think we even deserve merciful lovingkindness. Maybe we agree with those who say we need to be punished (especially if we've begun to seek spiritual sobriety). Maybe we're

---

6. Romans 7:18–20 NLT.

so tired of trying to stop our addictive behaviors that we figure we might as well go full speed ahead.

One thing is true for most addicts: we won't stop until something stops us.

Mental illness stopped me. In some strange way, accepting help for my depression was exactly the act of difficult kindness that my sick self needed. It was the first step toward acknowledging that I had needs without shaming myself for having them.

Accepting help for my depression was also the first step toward accepting my religious addiction. Acknowledging the reality of my mental illness and realizing it wasn't my fault prepared me to identify as a religious addict—which was just another kind of illness. Depression was my *misericord*: a compassionate dagger that delivered the mercy stroke, ending my denial. Accepting the reality of my illness was an important step in my spiritual sobriety, because in that acceptance I found the *misercord* of God: His kindness leading to my repentance.[7]

What about you? Can you identify anyone or anything that might be acting as a *misercord* in your life? Is an issue trying to draw your attention to your addiction? If so, take a look. Let the mercy stroke do its work. Let compassion point you in a better direction.

7. Romans 2:4, NASB.

Being Sick and Getting Well

I can think of few other illnesses that have the same kind of stigma as depression and mental illness. We RAs just don't like talking about it. We prefer talking about weak faith, doubt, and disobedience. We talk about trusting Jesus, writing gratitude journals, and praying more as a way to "increase joy."

And outside of church, our culture tells us to hide weakness, too. There is relentless pressure to "live the best life," to "give 110 percent," to "go big or go home." Our society is obsessed with prowess. Everyone from helicopter pilots to athletic coaches, corporate executives to lower management are all driven by a need to be in control, winning, growing profit, and producing. Sometimes it feels as though the worst sin you can commit is to be mediocre. Or to have a problem like depression.

In response to a question I posed on Facebook, a woman named Martha shared how her church responded to her husband's depression. "My husband has severe mental illness. For years he was told that if he could repent he would get better. When he was hospitalized and medicated, it was a wonderful blessing but I couldn't share it with my church because their judgment was more than I could bear."[8]

Laura had a similar experience. "In our ultraconservative church, my parents were told that my physical and mental problems would get better if they just had more faith. I have been struggling with depression, anxiety, and PTSD for the

---

8. "Why Is There So Much Stigma Attached to Christians Accepting Help for Mental Illness?" Online interview by author. April 20, 2015.

last thirty years. The diagnosis of PTSD was *so very* freeing for me and helped me start healing."[9]

And yes, Christians can suffer from PTSD after a traumatic church experience and after becoming or living among religious addicts. Author and blogger Reba Riley calls it Post-Traumatic Church Syndrome (PTCS):

> There are degrees of PTCS—maybe you can still walk into a church, maybe you can't. . . . But the one thing we all have in common is that we crash into religion when we go looking for God. And the crashing has left us with spiritual whiplash, broken bones, bruises, welts and lacerations. It has left us feeling alone and scared and suffering. It has left us with a boatload of internal and external symptoms [that] persons of spiritual authority tell us are all in our heads and would go away if we just had more faith. . . . I can tell you there are thousands, maybe even millions of us. I can tell you that I recovered, that healing is available, that God will meet you wherever you are or aren't.[10]

In my case, it took me almost forty years to get my chronic depression and PTCS diagnosed. It took that long because I didn't think they existed.

---

9. "Why Is There So Much Stigma Attached to Christians Accepting Help for Mental Illness?" Online interview by author. April 20, 2015.

10. Reba Riley, "It's Called Post-Traumatic Church Syndrome, and Yes It's Real," Patheos/Faith Forward (blog), March 5, 2014. http://www.patheos.com/blogs/faithforward/2014/03/its-called-post-traumatic-church-syndrome-and-yes-its-real/#ixzz3YjiKJjykE.

Even as the stigma surrounding mental illness has lessened, many Christians still refuse to view illness as real and not a matter of holiness. If they did, they wouldn't advise their depressed friends to just go for a walk and count their blessings. If a friend has cancer, we want him or her to seek medical care and drug-based therapies. But if a friend has mental illness, RAs often suggest he or she try prayer, essential oils, St. John's Wort—anything other than medical help. They may even suggest their friend's mental illness is the result of sin.

Angel, a young woman who was diagnosed with mental illness as a teenager, told me her parents refused medical care for her because they believed she just needed to repent. "My parents thought I was being rebellious and living in sin; hence the depression," Angel wrote. "They wouldn't allow me to take medication."[11]

Kay Bruner, a therapist and author, says this kind of belief is common among Christians. "It's easier to blame people for not being spiritual enough than to actually stick in there while they do the messy work of healing. I grew up in a family where a lot of us self-medicated for mental illness with alcohol or religion. It was easier to wave the spiritual magic wand than do the true work that recovery requires."[12]

11. "Why Is There So Much Stigma Attached to Christians Accepting Help for Mental Illness?" Online interview by author. April 20, 2015.

12. "Quote for Your Book." E-mail message to author. April 20, 2015.

Naming the Shadow

My own family history is rife with mental illness—most of it unacknowledged and undiagnosed. I never talked about this very real health issue with my parents until after I'd received my diagnosis. But it was all there. As soon as I named the shadow that had haunted me, suddenly I began recognizing it in other family members. Why did my maternal grandmother lock herself away for days at a time? Why didn't we ever talk about my paternal grandmother's sister—the one who committed suicide? Why didn't the delusional teachings of my cult-founding grandfather ever give us pause? Why did my uncle have such out-of-control rage issues? Why did we all pretend everything was fine?

Talking about mental illness means getting real: acknowledging the presence of something inexplicable. And we RAs don't really believe in the inexplicable. There's an answer for *everything*—usually with a Bible verse or doctrinal belief attached to it. If the illness doesn't line up with what we believe, then it isn't valid.

A mom named Sarah shared with me how these kinds of beliefs prevented her from getting the help she needed after giving birth. "When I was clinically depressed post-partum, my husband—an all-around good guy!—reinforced my refusal of psychiatric therapies because it didn't fit with his idea of how God works. He really believed God wouldn't allow a person to be afflicted with a condition that compromises one's free will."[13]

---

13. "Why Is There So Much Stigma Attached to Christians Accepting Help for Mental Illness?" Online interview by author. April 20, 2015.

I understand why we don't talk about mental illness. We fear it. It doesn't feel manageable like other diseases. There are no vaccines. It isn't predictable. And courses of treatment aren't standardized. It's *too* real. We don't talk about depression or anxiety, because we can't contain it with words and thereby control it. It reminds us too much of our human limitations, our powerlessness. It makes us feel helpless—and helplessness is the one thing we can-do religious addicts avoid at all costs.

But what if helplessness is exactly what we need?

What if admitting we need help is the doorway to a new, healthy relationship with God and the world around us?

Or maybe we're just so worn out and done with the whole God thing that we need to walk away completely. That's okay. Sometimes the very best thing we can do for our spiritual recovery is to give ourselves permission to stop trying. God is big enough to meet us anywhere.

Whatever your situation, surrender. Get help if you need it. Face your reality and become spiritually sober.

A Stretcher from Grace

In his poem "Zero Circle," the thirteenth-century Persian poet Rumi described a state of being that is conducive to transformation. It is a place beyond thinking, beyond evaluation, beyond critique:

> *Be helpless, dumbfounded,*
> *Unable to say yes or no.*

Then a stretcher will come from grace
To gather us up.[14]

When faced with the uncontrollable compulsion that is our disease, aren't we utterly dumbfounded? There is no rhyme or reason for why we do what we do. We can't explain it with words. According to the *Big Book of Alcoholics Anonymous*, this is because we are dealing with addiction, a disease that is "baffling, cunning, powerful! Without help it is too much for us."[15]

For those of us steeped in the subculture of compulsive Christianity, admitting we've made a mess of our spirituality feels like a failure of our faith. Since much of evangelical Christian culture emphasizes personal knowledge of Scripture and readiness to defend one's beliefs, admitting we need help feels like a betrayal of our "Christian example." Similarly, the broader societal pressure to be in control, to keep up appearances, to achieve upward mobility so strongly defines our individual worth that we don't know how to cope when things don't feel right.

Here's the good news: We don't have to lose relationships, jobs, or churches before we admit we have a problem with the way we use God, religion, and our belief systems. We simply need to be *willing*.

In her book *Living Beautifully with Uncertainty and*

14. Roger Housden, *Ten Poems to Change Your Life* (New York: Harmony Books, 2001), 43.

15. Dr. Bob Smith and Bill Wilson, *The Big Book of Alcoholics Anonymous* (Lark Publishing LLC, 2013), 32.

Change, Pema Chödrön writes, "We need to ask ourselves if we're *ready* to do something different. Are we sick to death of the same old repetitive patterns? Do we want to allow the space for new possibilities to emerge?"[16]

Sit with that for a moment. How do you feel about your old, repetitive patterns? Can you see them? Are you ready for new possibilities to emerge? Lena, a recovering food addict, offers a suggestion for gauging willingness: "Are you ready to be done?"

This isn't a judgmental question or even a question about our specific behaviors. It's just a question about whether we're ready to stop spending all of our energy trying to hide that we have a problem. It's a question that provides dignity to us addicts—even when we're not sober—because it tells us we still have choices, we can still choose our response, and we are not lost causes.

Perhaps we also need to ask ourselves what obstacles are preventing us from being willing: perfectionism (wanting to have a superclean, no-mistakes life), either/or thinking (believing there is only one right answer or way of doing things), procrastination, fear of identity loss (who are we without our habits and rituals, our superhuman efforts to be spiritual giants?), waiting for others to rescue us, or being so consumed with rescuing others that we permanently delay saving ourselves.

16. Pema Chödrön, *Living Beautifully with Uncertainty and Change* (Boston, MA: Shambhala, 2013), 52.

The Way of Littleness

In his book *Abide in Christ*, Andrew Murray writes, "It is not the yoke but the resistance to the yoke that makes the difficulty; the whole-hearted surrender . . . finds and secures the rest."[17] Have you considered that maybe your resistance to willingness is more painful than the changes you need to make? As the old adage goes: "Pain is inevitable, but suffering is optional."

So, what does it mean to be willing? What does it look like?

I believe willingness is the way of littleness.

Willing people see themselves in right proportion to their disease and to God. In other words, we first recognize that our addictive behaviors are bigger than our ability to control them, and second, we learn to see God as being bigger than both our disease *and* us.

St. Thérèse of Lisieux, the young nun famous for developing "the little way," of Spirituality, once wrote: "I would . . . like to find an elevator to lift me up to Jesus, because I'm too little to climb the rough staircase of perfection."[18]

When we've been trapped in a pattern of addictive behavior, it is a huge relief to admit we are little, our addiction is big, and we need a Jesus Elevator to lift us to sobriety. Getting in touch with our littleness, then, is not an exercise in self-degradation but rather an exercise in affirmation. When we acknowledge our littleness we are simply acknowledging

17. Andrew Murray, *Abide in Christ* (New York: Grosset & Dunlap, 1888), 22.

18. St. Thérèse of Lisieux, *The Story of a Soul: A New Translation*, trans. Robert Edmonson (Brewster, MA: Paraclete Press, 2006), 230–31.

the way things are, and this kind of honesty *always* benefits our sense of self-worth. Most of us have been struggling for so long to climb the "rough staircase" on our own that by the time an elevator shows up, we're so exhausted we don't need persuading. We crash-land onto that Jesus Elevator, Christian reputation or not.

If you're anything like me, willingness doesn't come easily. But it can happen a little more freely if we let it. Jane, a sober alcoholic and recovering love addict, once told me that sometimes we need to pray for the "willingness to be willing."[19]

I've found hope in recovery texts that say, "Even the smallest amount of willingness opens the door to the power of God's healing."[20] Perhaps, as with faith, all we need is willingness the size of a mustard seed. And when that tiny seed is planted in our hearts and reality confronts us, God's *misericordia* will come like the spring rain, watering our souls into flourishing spiritual sobriety.

Practice Your Spiritual Sobriety

Prayer:

> *God, help me see that my weaknesses are not liabilities but rather opportunities and instruments of your misericordia. May I embrace the way of littleness and willingly receive the "stretcher from grace" that can gather me up into your everlasting love.*

19. "Working the Twelve Steps." Telephone interview by author. January 5, 2015.

20. Co-Dependents Anonymous, Inc., *Co-dependents Anonymous* (Phoenix, AZ: Co-Dependents Anonymous, Inc., 2nd ed., 2008), 52.

Promise:

"But he said to me, 'My grace is sufficient for you, for my power is made perfect in weakness.' Therefore, I will boast all the more gladly about my weaknesses, so that Christ's power may rest on me. That is why, for Christ's sake, I delight in weaknesses, in insults, in hardships, in persecutions, in difficulties. For when I am weak, then I am strong." 2 Corinthians 12:9-10, NIV

Journaling/Group Questions:

- Early in this chapter a woman named Laura shared that she had to stop attending conferences because the religious high translated into depression when she got home. Have you ever been inspired by a conference or speaker and then been unable to sustain that emotional high once you got home? Have your expectations and hopes for building a thriving spirituality ever been disappointed by the realities and responsibilities of everyday life? Explain.

- When I left the cult at age twenty-five, I felt disconnected from church and mainstream society. I felt like I didn't fit in. Have you ever felt this way at church or among your peers? How have you tried to "fit in"? Share about a time in your life when you felt like an outsider. How can being honest about our weaknesses help our spiritual sobriety?

- St. Paul says, "I want to do what is good, but I don't. I don't want to do what is wrong, but I do it anyway." Can you relate to this feeling? Have you ever felt your "sick self" forcing you to do the things you don't want to do? Name some habits you've tried to quit but can't stop doing. Why is it helpful to view our compulsive, addictive behavior as a disease?

- In this chapter, several people shared how their families and churches believed mental illness was the result of sin or weak faith. Have you ever experienced something similar? Did this affect your relationship with God or the church? Therapist and author Kay Bruner pointed out that "it's easier to blame people for not being spiritual enough than to actually stick in there while they do the messy work of healing." Describe a time in your life when someone stuck by your side. List the qualities of this friend: i.e., loving, patient, compassionate, empathetic. Now imagine that God embodies all these qualities. Would that change your relationship with God? How so?

3

Rehab for Junkies

Searching for the Real God

Religious addicts feel judged by God—so they learn to judge.
Religious addicts feel that God sees them as dirty and sinful—so
they make others feel dirty and sinful. Religious addicts feel like
victims of God's whims—so they victimize and abuse others.

—*FATHER LEO BOOTH*

YEARS AGO, WHEN I LEFT MY FAMILY'S CULT, I FOUND MY-self having a God crisis.

Or maybe it was a nervous breakdown. I didn't know. All I knew was that even though I'd accepted help for my depression and begun to embrace spiritual sobriety, I seemed to have lost God again. Daily medication was rehabilitating my mental health, but daily interactions with God were damaging my spiritual health.

Where expressions of faith were once food to my soul, now they fed only the emptiness I felt. Where prayer was once a comfort, it was now a confusing effort to reach someone I wasn't sure I wanted to know. Where devotions had meant communion with my Savior, now they felt futile and meaningless. God was letting me down in every encounter.

Before acknowledging my addiction, I thought that for good things to happen in my life, I just needed to believe harder. But now that I was discovering that so many of my previous beliefs were false and destructive, I was beginning to wonder if my actual concept of God was healthy. I had to ask myself, What if my understanding of God isn't good for my spirituality? What if I need to lose a false God in order to find the real one?

Suddenly, nothing—religious activity or regular activity—seemed to be working. My God-need was being swallowed up by my addict-need. And my addictions had spread.

In my case, using God addictively turned into my gateway drug to a whole bunch of other harmful habits. I'd chased the religious glory-feeling for so long that it was easy to transfer that compulsive behavior to other things, including (but certainly not limited to) my iPhone, Facebook, Twitter, Christian conferences, texting, blogging, blogging conferences, obsessing about other bloggers, podcasts, work, arguing on the Internet, Instagram, sarcasm, the Food Network, reality TV, Diet Coke, Cookie Butter, Mint Milanos, political commentary, being the best mother ever, fabric, yarn, French country décor, doomsday prepping, being right, being liked, looking up DIY chicken coops on Pinterest, controlling all things, extreme couponing—not to mention my short-lived but totally weird obsession with porcelain dolls. (*Ew.*)

But just as my addiction to religious activity, rituals, and emotionalism always led to a letdown, despair, and self-loathing, so my addiction to certain compulsive habits led to experiencing even more defeat and addictive behavior. Because, of course, none of these substitute activities brought any lasting relief. They just kept me distracted from the pain of becoming sober—which hindered my success in becoming sober.

You might be asking what Facebook and porcelain dolls

have to do with one's spiritual life, and in particular our desire to have a healthier one. All of this began with God—or rather with the way I used God. Religious addiction and harmful habits are related: they both spring from our human need for connection, comfort, meaning, transcendence. Our compulsions are often sourced in spiritual, emotional emptiness: destructive patterns can be driven by yearnings that are more religious than we realize. Activity addicts try to fill a spiritual need with something physical. Some of us might move from using religion as an escape to using almost any activity to treat the same longings—and we suffer as a result.

Spiritual sobriety isn't just for religious addicts. It's for habit addicts, too.

Think about this for a minute. Can you identify any habits that have metamorphosed into fixations in ways that rival your religious addiction? Have any fun or stress-relieving activities become threatening to your well-being, your relationships, your attempts to live a sober, healthy life?

As with religious addiction, I've created a list of symptoms for those struggling with compulsive activities. See if any of this sounds familiar.

CHARACTERISTICS OF HABIT ADDICTION

1. We show an inability to stop a compulsive behavior, even in the face of increasingly negative consequences.
2. We exhibit behavior marked by impulsivity or obsession.
3. We exhibit behavior consistently motivated by stress, anger, sadness, isolation, unmet expectations, neglected needs, or a sense of entitlement.

4. We show an excessive reliance on quick relief instead of long-term, positive change.
5. We have an inability to acknowledge the negative impact of our harmful habits on ourselves and others.

For me, the little pleasures that were once a welcome escape morphed into a whole lifestyle of obsessive distraction. I wanted unconditional love, but I settled for a few Facebook likes and a couple dozen retweets; I wanted fullness of joy, but I settled for filling my belly with Cookie Butter; I needed authentic connection, but I traded that for one more social media app; I wanted to change the world, but I was content just to argue on the Internet. All I'd wanted was affirmation, validation, a way to soothe the daily difficulties of this unwieldy life.

Don't we all need that?

But eventually, despite my pursuit of spiritual sobriety, I found myself constantly exhausted, irritated, anxious, and short-tempered. I routinely left tasks half-finished, laundry washed but not dried, appointments missed, children waiting at school. . . . How did this happen? How did my life become a consistently dissatisfying and painful whirlwind?

Finally I did what any smart junkie does.

Rehab Bound

"We have a spot open next week, and we can offer you a partial scholarship," the kind woman at Five Sisters Ranch had told me over the phone. This wasn't a traditional rehab, she said. It was more like a two-week spiritual retreat center that helped women heal from codependency and addictive behaviors.

I booked the spot. If nothing else, I needed a break from my fast-paced life. I needed rest. I needed time away from all the habits I'd been leaning on to distract me from the hard work I needed to do. I had begun to mentally connect my frantic activities with my religious addiction—same root, different behavior—and had begun to realize that these substitutes for God weren't fitting the bill. I had to face the next step in my sobriety: finding God again. Not the judgmental God of my fathers and not the God-drug I'd used for so long—but a real, loving God.

I didn't know if that was possible.

I wasn't sure such a God existed.

The experience was, at first, terrifying. "Can't I just have my iPhone at nights before I go to bed?" I asked the intake person at the retreat center.

She chuckled, then locked my iPhone in a closet.

Hey, if you're wondering whether you're addicted to something, try quitting it cold turkey. See if you can live *comfortably* without it. Sobriety isn't about white-knuckling your way through two weeks without texting, for example. That's called *fasting*. Rather, the truly sober person can, somewhat serenely, let go indefinitely. Take it or leave it. This is what saints and mystics often refer to as *detachment*, and it's pretty much the hardest thing ever.

I had a headache. I felt like vomiting. My skin itched. It was as if the protective coating of my soul was rubbed raw and I was all exposed, nerves blanching in the sudden, unforgiving light. I even seemed to have lost my words and could hardly speak.

A line by Sylvia Plath floated through my addled mind: "This is the silence of astounded souls."[1]

At dinner, I picked up my fork and it clattered on the plate. I couldn't swallow.

"You're in withdrawal," explained a counselor as she placed a soft, gentle hand on my forearm. "Can you look at me?"

I wrenched my head up and looked into her crinkly, smiling eyes.

"You're safe here," she said. "This is a safe place to fall apart."

The other women who were there for treatment grew quiet. But it was a healing silence. It did not judge. It was still. It calmly held the space while I got to sit quietly and "feel the uncomfortable feelings," as the counselors said. In other words, I got to feel all the things I'd been avoiding feeling for the past several years and even recently as I fought my addictions. Yay, sobriety.

Stopping addictive behaviors even temporarily felt impossible. Give them up permanently? How was I supposed to live the rest of my life without getting high on my religion *or* my habits? And why should I?

When I asked one of the therapists this question, she smiled mysteriously and said, "Because sobriety is more satisfying."

I hated her.

---

1. Sylvia Plath, "Crossing the Water." In *Plath: Poems*, edited by Diane Wood Middlebrook (New York: Knopf, 1998), 147.

Horse Time

"We don't break our horses," Alyssa said, "we invite them into partnership with us." Her bright eyes sparkled beneath the broad brim of her cowboy hat.

It was my fifth day at the treatment center, and we'd been standing on the windswept hill for what seemed like an eternity doing nothing but watching horses. Horses standing. Horses grazing. Horses *flicking their tails*. Alyssa told us that being still this way was an exercise in developing our inner observer.

I didn't know what I was supposed to be observing other than my raging boredom. Being still is damn uncomfortable. Did I mention boring?

"You're on horse time now," Alyssa said. "For those of us accustomed to rushing around, this is really difficult. When I first started working with horses, I couldn't sit still for more than five minutes."

I shifted my weight from foot to foot, balled my hands into fists, and pushed them into the pockets of my windbreaker. I didn't understand how you were supposed to control a horse without breaking her, and I certainly didn't understand how being on horse time had anything to do with pursuing sobriety and reconciling my relationship to God.

Still, there was something about Alyssa's way of being that intrigued me. She was loose and easeful. She walked gently, slowly, and intentionally. She talked casually to her horses as if they understood English. I had no idea how this worked, but it was obvious the horses connected with her because they responded to her. They routinely obeyed Alyssa's instructions. They watched her placidly. They submitted to her touch without fear.

I was utterly baffled. This was a language I didn't understand. I was not accustomed to tenderness, partnership, and relationships between equals. My relationship with God was black-and-white, hierarchal, and based on fear. The language Alyssa shared with her horses was utterly foreign to me. She asked her horses into partnership; she didn't force them. Her tone was soft and respectful. But I could see the results: mutual respect and implicit trust. *This must be what love looks like*, I thought.

At one point, Alyssa brought a horse to me. She asked if I'd like to brush the horse's mane.

"Uh . . . no thanks."

The horse was huge. One kick from those hooves and I'd be dead.

Alyssa smiled and showed me how to hold the brush, how to approach the horse—almost asking its permission before touching—and then how to gently stroke the long, coarse mane. She held out the brush.

"This is an experience you need to have. Your discomfort wants to teach you something. Maybe it's time to stop running from your fear of feeling difficult feelings. Allow yourself to welcome the pain and sit with it."

Uh-huh, gotcha. Welcome the pain. Again. Are you kidding?

I couldn't believe I was paying money to brush tangles out of a horse's mane. I brushed tangled kid hair at home every day.

Still, I took a hesitant step toward the horse. She turned her head at the sound of my footfall and suddenly I was looking into the liquid brown depths of her eye. In my peripheral vision, I saw one of her ears cock forward. I heard a tail gently flick.

From somewhere behind me, Alyssa said, "Yes, you connected! She's saying okay. Step forward and reach for the top of her mane."

She said okay? How do you know she didn't say, Get the hell back?

But I inched a little closer and reached for the top of the horse's mane anyway. It was wiry and coarse beneath my fingers. The lush smell of her animal body rose up around me. I edged closer to the long, muscular plane of her neck. I blinked and crinkled my nose, trying to assimilate this overwhelming sensory experience.

"Begin brushing," Alyssa quietly urged.

I lifted the brush to the horse's mane, and suddenly, I was transported to my kitchen at home, brushing my twins' hair before school—

"Ow, Mommy! Ow! That *hurted*!"

"Sorry but we're in a hurry," said a harsh, harried voice inside my mind—

I shook my head, snapping myself back to the barn, back to the horse in front of me.

"We don't have to hurry," I whispered to the horse, to myself, to my little girls back home. "It doesn't have to hurt. We're on horse time now."

I took a deep breath and slowed myself down. I brushed smoothly and rhythmically. I took my time. I felt myself relax.

"Good, Elizabeth," said Alyssa from somewhere behind me. "Now, it's time to detach."

I froze. *Detach? But I just got here! This horse and I are having an experience! I could stay here all day!*

I placed a hand on the horse's neck and patted it once, twice. Then I stepped back.

Strangely, I started to cry. I gave the brush back to Alyssa and turned away, not wanting her to see my tears. I took my seat beside the other women from our treatment house.

And that's when I saw the connection. I saw that my default was frantic hurry. I saw that my relationship with God wasn't a partnership but one based on fear of punishment. No wonder I'd felt abandoned by God: I couldn't trust Him enough to let Him love me. No wonder I sought relief in secretive behaviors: when I couldn't find the love I needed from God, I tried to find it elsewhere.

What if a deep-seated belief in my inherent wickedness was the perfect setup for my addictive behaviors? What if shame begets shameful behavior?

Maybe everybody needs to experience the unconditional love of God before he or she can get better.

If the first step of spiritual sobriety is admitting we have a problem with the way we use God and the second is facing reality, then perhaps the third is coming to believe that a loving God exists and that he can restore us to sanity and sobriety.

Who Is God for You?

Developing a healthy relationship with God was and continues to be the most difficult aspect of my recovery. It has required a near total deconstruction of everything I thought I knew about faith. As a female raised in a highly patriarchal church culture, I was taught that my father was God for me and, later, my husband was. This idea—that a human being represents God for you—is a dangerous lie, because if someone controls your concept of God, he controls *everything*.

When I was growing up, my life revolved around trying harder to be good and perfect, "without spot or blemish." I controlled every aspect of my life by following a rigid schedule, becoming scrupulous and harshly critical about my personal appearance, my body, my daily schedule, and my confession lists. Still, I never measured up.

I rarely spoke directly to anyone. I hinted, suggested, or spoke in a baby voice. I hedged. I equivocated. I watched my parents' moods closely before asking for what I needed or wanted. When someone treated me abusively, I adopted coping mechanisms like avoidance. I never confronted abusive treatment, and I even avoided my own feelings about it.

But all the control and scrupulosity didn't take away my deep, real need for love. Once out of the cult, I turned my focus to relationships: seeking friendships and romantic love that would fulfill, heal, and make me whole. My emotional intensity enabled me to become deeply intimate with people very quickly. But when someone got too close, I pulled away—true intimacy was terrifying. I was afraid everyone was abusive.

Over time, I transferred my abusers' traits to my concept of God. The God I knew was wrathful and harsh. The God I knew hadn't protected me from people who hurt me. The God I knew was stone silent in the face of my desperate prayers. I began to believe that I was unlovable and inherently bad. I certainly didn't deserve love—I had to earn it. Love was given or withheld based on my level of submission. *If I disobey I will be disowned.*

Others cling desperately to the idea of a God who will magically grant their wishes—often until a moment of crisis smashes that idea into pieces. For Mary Jo, that crisis was the sudden, unexpected death of her husband. She shared,

> We had hard times, but Jesus was always the victor and things worked out. And then Martin died. Our prayers in the emergency room were answered with a big, resounding no! Now, my quest is to find the true nature of God. Not the stand-in-a-prayer-circle-around-the-vending-machine-and-press-B3-to-get-exactly-what-we-asked-for God.[2]

This is such a painful place for a Christian to find herself, isn't it? I've done the same thing Mary Jo did—used God like a vending machine, unwilling to admit there was a problem with that.

Who Is Your Higher Power?

Once I was seeking spiritual sobriety, though, I routinely made other people, places, pursuits, and things my higher power. (Hence the issues with Facebook and porcelain dolls.) If only I had a best friend, life would be meaningful! If only we moved to the country, I would feel whole! If only people

2. "From Vending Machine God." E-mail message to author. April 20, 2015.

loved me the way I wanted them to love me, I would feel loved! If only I had a successful career and a fat bank account, I would feel safe!

I didn't know it at the time, but by making other people, places, pursuits, and things my higher power, and by not allowing myself to develop a new understanding of God, I was actually retraumatizing myself. And I was avoiding finding a real God.

Take a minute to think about this. Have you replaced your higher power with a compulsive habit? Or if God is still your higher power, has a wrong belief about Him corrupted your relationship with Him? Remember, your sobriety depends on your honesty and willingness to face reality.

It became clear to me that a full recovery meant confronting my root issue: my unhealthy view of God. That was the core of my religious and habit addiction. I knew that if I was ever to live a healthy, happy life, I desperately needed a safe and loving higher power.

What I didn't know was how hard that was to find.

According to Dr. Robert Stuckey, whose rehab centers have treated thousands, the recovery rate is much lower for addicts who have a fearful and punishing view of God. In fact, they "have a harder time than people with no religious training at all."[3]

Another recovery specialist, Dr. Patrick Carnes, reports that recent findings in neuroscience tell us a sense of safety is essential for healing the brain. We can't force ourselves

3. Dr. Robert Stuckey, MD, "You Gotta Have Hope," *New Catholic World* 232, no. 1390 (July/August, 1989). As quoted by Dennis Linn, *Good Goats: Healing Our Image of God* (Mahwah, NJ: Paulist Press, 1994), 45.

into healing because "only when the brain feels safe can it optimally reconstruct itself. It needs to know that it is being understood and empathized with."[4] We feel safe when we are accepted—warts and all—without judgment. We feel safe when we don't have to perform as the Good Christian or the hotshot in the office but can simply be human. We feel safe in the presence of nonjudgmental compassion.

And only when we are in this safe space can we relax and open ourselves to "optimal reconstruction." But even that requires courage! In religiously addictive environments we were specifically warned *against* developing our own concept of God because we might end up forming God in our own image—idolatry!

"Like many people from legalistic backgrounds, I heard sermons about how evil, corrupt people worship a God of their own creation," said Jackie. "I am weary of that. I think a person's spiritual journey is taken in a variety of ways. Mine is still 'to be continued.'"[5]

It's difficult to take our own journeys when some of the most popular Christian recovery programs discourage us from developing our own understanding of God. For example, some bestselling books change the wording of the Twelve Steps to better fit Christian doctrine. In the original Twelve Steps of Alcoholics Anonymous, Step Three reads: "We made a decision to turn our wills and our lives over to

4. Partick Carnes, *A Gentle Path Through the Twelve Steps* (Center City, MN: Hazelden, 2012), 9.

5. "Have You Ever Had to Reconfigure Your Understanding of God?" Online interview by author. April 21, 2015.

the care of God as we understood Him."[6] But a Christian recovery resource omits the phrase "as we understood Him."[7] Presumably, religious addicts are allowed to turn their wills and lives over only to a collectively agreed upon Christian God. And this can actually do more damage to those of us who were told the Christian God is relentlessly judgmental.

I think there's an important reason the authors of *The Big Book of Alcoholics Anonymous* included that phrase. They understood that for some people to achieve healing and recovery, they needed the freedom to experience God outside traditional religious structures.

The point of recovery is *healing*, not making sure everyone's understanding of God is the same.

Reimagining God

In his book, *Good Goats: Healing Our Image of God*, author and therapist Dennis Linn writes, "We become like the God we adore."[8] If we are to achieve spiritual sobriety and live successful, productive lives, we need to meet a God who tells us we're unconditionally loved and infinitely valued, no matter what we do, accomplish, or feel in one particular moment.

"I am still trying to do this," Heather wrote in response to a survey about this topic. "It's really hard. If I admit that

6. Alcoholics Anonymous World Services, Inc., *Twelve Steps and Twelve Traditions* (New York: Alcoholics Anonymous World Services, Inc., 1981), 5.

7. Stephen Arterburn and David Stoop, *The Book of Life Recovery: Inspiring Stories and Biblical Wisdom for Your Journey Through the Twelve Steps* (Carol Stream, IL: Tyndale Momentum, 2012), vii.

8. Linn, *Good Goats,* 42.

what I was taught about God is wrong, then what else from my childhood might not be true? Faith was in every aspect of my childhood—which was great in so many ways—but it also distorted a lot of things for me."[9]

We might even need to take a break from God altogether. "For years I acted as an atheist," Sandra wrote on my Facebook page.

> I didn't want to make something up to replace what I couldn't accept. So I acted as if there were no God. Looking back, I realize that I left it up to God to reveal God to me. I didn't seek God, didn't want to reinvent God, but I remained open to being sought by God. It took several years of interactions with this Reality before I even recognized it as God but when I did, wow.
>
> One day, during a moment of meditation after yoga, I was engulfed by Something Other. I experienced a communion so fully accepting, so completely loving, so infinitely boundless and compassionate that I barely noticed when I lost myself in it. I was still so trapped in my fundamentalist understanding that I couldn't begin to call that experience God, but I knew I had experienced grace.
>
> Eventually, through my reading of mystics— Christian, Muslim, Hindu, and others—combined with my study of shamanism, paganism, and ancient Christianity, I began to accept that this Grace, this Love that

9.　"Have You Ever Had to Reconfigure Your Understanding of God?" Online interview by author. April 21, 2015.

sought and found me, was best known as God. I was indeed wooed by Love.[10]

Sandra's story gives me such hope. She did something vital: she gave herself permission to just be, to remain open. She stopped trying to figure everything out, to form definitions, and she let whatever needed to be revealed be revealed. That takes guts.

I've found that reimaging God can be as difficult or easy as I allow it to be. For example, I make my spirituality unnecessarily difficult when I take a Scripture out of context and claim it as a promise for my life. When God doesn't make this promise come true for me, I can either sit there banging my head against my Bible and asking God, "Why isn't this working?" Or I can admit I pulled that verse out of context. Other times, I complicate my relationship with God by worrying that I'm just making things up. What if my understanding of God isn't *true*?

When I'm getting all freaked out—*Oh my God, what if my God isn't God?*—I ask myself one question: Do I want answers or do I want serenity? That usually calms me down and helps me recognize those scared, angry voices are from my past. They no longer represent my voice or God's. As Rabbi Rami Shapiro writes, "If your understanding of God allows you to recover from your addiction and brings some sanity to your life, then your God is as true as God needs to be."[11]

10. "Have You Ever Had to Reconfigure Your Understanding of God?" Online interview by author. April 21, 2015.

11. Rami Shapiro, *Recovery—The Sacred Art* (Woodstock, VT: SkyLight Paths Publishing, 2009), 42.

Whoa. Heresy alert, right?

I get it. Here's the thing: I don't fault any addict whose recovery hinges upon needing the God of his or her understanding to be the true God as defined by his or her religion. When people are freshly getting sober, some don't feel safe unless they belong to a group of people who are similar to them. They can't tolerate much difference of belief about God, political ideals, or even public school vs. private school. So, if that's what you need to feel safe, too, then that's what you use for your recovery. There are lots of recovery groups whose members agree upon the same definition of God.

Remember that your recovery is as unique as you are. You don't have to wait until everyone is in agreement (or grants you permission) before you seek the healing you need. A big part of recovery is taking responsibility for what is yours and letting go of what is not. Other people's beliefs are not your responsibility, and your beliefs are not theirs, either. If we know the path we need to take, we don't need to wait for others to join us. We can start now.

A woman named Lissa, not a religious addict but someone rebuilding her faith, said this:

> I just don't know what a faith expression looks like for me anymore. I've taken a hiatus from trying to decide what I believe, because so much of what I considered faith was just a collection of theories about God. Real faith is something else entirely, and I'd like to find ways to experience the essence of faith in new ways. . . . I tried hard not to believe in God at all, but I just couldn't pull it off. I

couldn't tell you who God is, or how God really operates in the world anymore, but I can't shake the belief that there is one.[12]

Even if we are feeling confused, we can still turn our lives over to the care of God, because when we *act as if* God is loving, we give God a chance to prove that He is. This is how we learn what St. Francis de Sales knew: "He is within you, seeking your best happiness."[13]

Finding Commonality in Shared Pain

Whatever your addiction, religious or otherwise, healing is possible. Healing is available. We just need the willingness to admit our problems and ask for the courage to do the work of recovery. People often ask me where they should go to find healing. Most want to find a recovery program or support group that is specifically tailored to the needs of the religious or habit addict.

I understand the reluctance to join a secular or nonreligious specific recovery program. I, too, felt my issues wouldn't be adequately addressed alongside those of substance addicts. But now I tend to agree with experts who suggest religious addicts need to recover in secular programs.

Father Leo Booth, the priest who wrote the ground-

12. Kathy Escobar, *Faith Shift: Finding Your Way Forward When Everything You Believe Is Coming Apart* (New York: Convergent Books, 2014), 120.

13. St. Francis de Sales, *Introduction to the Devout Life* (France, 1609; New York: Random House, 2002), 81.

breaking book on religious addiction, *When God Becomes a Drug*, says,

> Religious addicts typically seek a way to feel superior, chosen and special. Separating them into their own [recovery] track only enables that arrogance and false sense of specialness to flourish and serves to further isolate them. Mainstreaming them with other patients helps break down those barriers. . . . I believe that having religious addicts . . . working through their issues with a group of patients whose addictions may vary can help those patients examine their own issues around religion. . . . Many religious addicts, moreover, suffer from other compulsions and addictions, such as eating disorders and sexual addiction. I believe these addictions are linked and should be treated alongside each other.[14]

After my time at Five Sisters Ranch, I bounced around to a bunch of different support groups, therapists, and twelve-step programs before someone finally pointed out to me that maybe the problem wasn't with the groups but with my need to find one that fit *me* perfectly. I have since realized that if I really want recovery I will get it. Yes, it's important to find a group that works well for us, but it's equally important that we learn to work well with the group. (There are exceptions—see chapter 6.)

14. Leo Booth, *When God Becomes a Drug: Breaking the Chains of Religious Addiction and Abuse* (Los Angeles: J.P. Tarcher, 1991), 250.

For me, programs like Codependents Anonymous and Sex & Love Addicts Anonymous offered something I hadn't found in church-based support groups: an opportunity to work my recovery alongside others who struggled with addiction, even if our religious beliefs weren't the same. We found commonality in our shared pain and brokenness. I found that I could actually be more honest in nonreligious support groups because I wasn't worried about tarnishing my good-Christian-girl reputation.

Indeed, for many religious and habit addicts, the measure and quality of our spiritual sobriety is proportionate to our acceptance of people with different beliefs and backgrounds. As we listen to the stories of other addicts, we may be surprised to find how often we relate. This sense of understanding can lead us out of isolation and help us realize that while we are no better or worse than others, we're also not alone.

And while God won't do our work for us (because a loving God respects our boundaries), when we do our part, God does His. Indeed, we will come to find—as a popular twelve-step affirmation says—that God does for us what we cannot do for ourselves. Spiritual sobriety begins when we admit we have a problem, and it continues when we identify and learn to live without the pursuits that compulsively control us. It grows as we redefine who God is and how he interacts with us.

Practice Your Spiritual Sobriety

Prayer:

> *God, help me understand and come to believe that you are FOR me, not against me. May I learn to trust that You are within me, seeking my "best happiness."*

Promise:

> " 'For I know the plans I have for you,' says the Lord. 'They are plans for good and not for disaster, to give you a future and a hope.' " Jeremiah 29:11, NLT

Let's take a closer look at the characteristics of habit addiction (pages 43–44). See where your behavior matches the descriptions. Record your answers in a journal. By the end of this exercise, you'll have insight into any destructive behaviors you may be practicing.

SYMPTOM #1: WE SHOW AN INABILITY TO STOP THE BEHAVIOR, EVEN IN THE FACE OF INCREASINGLY NEGATIVE CONSEQUENCES.

Explain how your habit has negatively impacted

- Your health (sleep loss, poor nutrition, lack of exercise, not getting regular dental and physical checkups, constant exhaustion).
- Your relationships (loss of intimacy, unresolved conflicts, neglecting responsibilities with spouse or children, broken friendships).
- Your career (arriving late, lower productivity, lack of focus, not completing tasks, always behind on work, unable to make quotas/reach goals).
- Your finances (poor credit, wasted money on habit, debt).

SYMPTOM #2: WE EXHIBIT BEHAVIOR MARKED BY IMPULSIVITY OR OBSESSION.

- Do you feel a strong, irresistible urge to engage your habit even when doing so is irrational or against your will?

- Do you act on your habit involuntarily? Do you find yourself acting out before you even realize what you're doing?
- When you have a free moment, do your thoughts immediately or frequently return to your addictive habit?

SYMPTOM #3: WE EXHIBIT BEHAVIOR CONSISTENTLY MOTIVATED BY STRESS, ANGER, SADNESS, ISOLATION, UNMET EXPECTATIONS, NEGLECTED NEEDS, OR A SENSE OF ENTITLEMENT.

- When you are experiencing negative emotions or "triggers," do you act out in your addictive habit more than you reach out for positive support?
- Do you feel shame and self-loathing after you've behaved addictively in response to negative emotions or triggers?

SYMPTOM #4: WE SHOW AN EXCESSIVE RELIANCE ON QUICK RELIEF INSTEAD OF LONG-TERM POSITIVE CHANGE.

- Have you ever ignored or postponed completing a task for so long that it creates new problems: i.e., not paying bills on time results in penalty fees, ignoring car problems results in major repairs?
- When has procrastination resulted in lost opportunities, missed appointments, or unfulfilled potential?

SYMPTOM #5: WE HAVE AN INABILITY TO ACKNOWLEDGE THE NEGATIVE IMPACT OF HARMFUL HABITS ON OURSELVES AND OTHERS.

- Have others expressed concern for your well-being?
- Have friends or loved ones attempted to help you stop your habit?
- Have you ever had thoughts that suggest you are "the exception" and won't experience the consequences of your behavior the way other addicts do?
- Do you minimize the negative impact of your addictive behavior?
- What are some excuses you've given for your behavior?

Again, if you recognize many of these behaviors and consequences, there's a good chance you're a habit addict. But again—good news! As you manage your sobriety, these other compulsions can be brought under control as well. Discipline has a way of spilling over into other areas.

In the pages ahead, my focus will be on RAs, but many of the ideas I suggest will apply to habit addicts as well. Keep reading!

4
Beautiful Humility

Developing a Sober Thought Life

A single footstep will not make a path on the earth, so a single thought will not make a pathway in the mind. To make a deep, physical path we walk again and again. To make a deep, mental path we must think over and over the kinds of thoughts we want to dominate our lives.

—*HENRY DAVID THOREAU*

JUST AS WORD AND ACTION ORIGINATE IN THOUGHT, SO also spiritual sobriety springs from the mind. The tricky part is developing an awareness of what we're thinking. Which thoughts are sober? Which are not? And furthermore, since we addicts are the ones doing the thinking, how can we identify our own damaging thoughts?

I would love to wake up each morning and have naturally occurring healthy thoughts. But since I'm a recovering religious addict, this is not my reality. Usually my eyes snap open a few minutes before my alarm goes off, and already, a bunch of anxious questions are stampeding through my head. *What day is it? What do I have to do today? What if the Rapture happens and I'm not ready? Do I feel joyful? Why don't I feel joyful? Where is God?*

It's almost as if my brain wakes up in a naturally occurring state of frenzy. Other religious addicts say they arise each morning full of self-doubt, convinced that no matter how hard they try to live a holy life, God will be displeased with them. Some say their minds are filled with thoughts about their own inferiority, a soundtrack on repeat that says they'll never measure up to the religious standards they once sought to emulate.

On the other hand, some of the religious addicts I knew while growing up often talked about waking up in a state of zealous excitement, jumping out of bed ready to live for God! Their naturally occurring state seemed to be manic self-confidence. But even though they claimed they'd found rest in Jesus, their lives were marked by restlessness—a kind of religious ADHD.

Likewise, the person addicted to harmful habits is driven by a compulsion to perform at work, keep up appearances with friends and neighbors, and acquire more followers on social media. None of these things is inherently bad, but the addict's obsessive behavior makes these good things destructive. Like the religious addict, the habit addict is forever chasing the next accolade or material reward and is never at peace.

Whether we wake full of self-doubt, zealous confidence, or unbridled ambition, the common denominator in all these thought patterns is a lack of calm, a lack of contentment with the present. Spiritual sobriety offers a different thought pattern: one that is at ease and at rest in the here and now.

Staying in the Here and Now

Like many addicts, I have a difficult time staying present. Left untended, my thoughts naturally slip away from me. The problem, of course, is that diligently disciplining our thoughts takes training. Ugh.

A recovering love addict named Laura spoke about how she deals with her runaway thinking: "If I want sober thoughts, I have to practice thinking them. It would be awesome to wake up one morning and be able to play Mozart. But life doesn't work that way and neither does sobriety. I can't expect to have a sane life if I'm not willing to practice sane thoughts and behavior."[1]

But how can we practice sane thoughts when the only thoughts we know are the frantic ones we're accustomed to thinking? Part of it is identifying the harmful, negative ones that no longer serve us and replacing those with new, healthy affirmations. It may feel bizarre at first, but writing a list of personal affirmations is one way to put new thoughts in our heads. Reading this list every morning is practicing sober thinking.

For example, a few of my most frequent negative thoughts are: *I am a bad person. I don't deserve love. I am not good enough.* So each morning I replace those negative thoughts with affirmations like these:

- I am loved.
- I am lovable.
- I am loving.
- I have everything I need.
- I am enough.

1. From a talk given on February 9, 2015, used with permission.

- I am doing my best and that's good enough.
- I am equal to the tasks set before me.
- I am becoming the person I was created to be.
- I am trustworthy.
- I am trusting myself to make healthy decisions.
- I am taking care of myself.
- I am courageous.
- I am allowed to enjoy my life.
- I am happy.
- I am safe.
- I am free.

Saying these statements aloud sometimes feels really awkward. But if my friends or children told me they had negative thoughts about themselves, I would tell them—without hesitation—that those thoughts are lies. The trouble is that when we're thinking those thoughts, they seem like truth! We have no trouble seeing all our mistakes and failures. We don't just think there's a log stuck in our eye; we're convinced there's an entire forest! I've discovered that repeating daily affirmations helps me balance my thoughts, even when saying them feels cheesy.

Simple and Earnest—and Short

Another important facet of sober thinking is prayer. Many religious addicts may need to start by relearning how to pray.

Spiritually sober prayers are shorter than the long, presumably "inspired" ones we heard while in addiction. Those of us from highly religious backgrounds may feel wary about short prayers, because we've been taught to equate them with laziness. But short prayers can help maintain focus (no time for daydreaming), keep things simple (no being long-winded or show-offy), and, most important, emphasize earnestness over wordiness. St. Francis de Sales suggests a manner of praying that is "not striving to say many words so much as a few words with your whole heart."[2]

Mary Jo, the new widow I mentioned earlier, shared that in her sober spiritual life she is "able to earnestly pray two prayers: 'Thank you' and 'Thy will be done.'"[3] You see? It doesn't have to be complicated. There is a beautiful humility in simple, earnest prayers. This is the kind of praying that heals religious addicts.

Still, praying simply and earnestly feels unnatural for some RAs because it's far different from how our religious leaders taught us to pray. Some said never to say the same prayer twice. We were supposed to come up with something entirely original every time we bowed our heads. In that way we would avoid "vain repetition."

Many RAs find help in written prayers. Amy shared with me that while seeking spiritual sobriety in college she was introduced to the Book of Common Prayer. "My prayers have never been the same! I love the rich language and feeling connected to all the people who have prayed the same thing."[4]

---

2. St. Francis de Sales, *Introduction to the Devout Life* (first published in 1609, France. New York: Random House, 2002), 48.

3. "What Are Some Funny/Odd Experiences You've Had While Praying?" Online interview by author. April 23, 2015.

4. Ibid.

Hazards of Prayer

If you grew up in evangelical Christianity, chances are you experienced the dangers of extemporaneous prayer. "Popcorn praying" happens when people in a group take turns praying aloud "as the Spirit leads."

But popcorn praying can be disastrous for RAs who use public supplication as a platform for attention-seeking or other odd prayer behaviors:

- Passive-aggressive prayers that shame someone in the room: "Lord, we pray for Sister Linda, who has been struggling with a bad attitude."
- Gossipy prayers about so-and-so's various sins: "Father, we lift up Brother Tom, who's struggling with impure thoughts."
- Preachy prayers that are basically full-length sermons.
- Scripture-infused prayers that highlight one's mastery of memorization.
- Bossy prayers telling God exactly what we want Him to do.

Looking back, I can see how those manners of praying exacerbated my religious addiction. It was startling to discover that sobriety programs suggest "praying *only* for knowledge of God's will for us and the power to carry that out."[5] As RAs, we're not interested in praying only for knowledge of God's will—where's the high in that? We have lots of other requests

---

5. Alcoholics Anonymous World Services, Inc., *Twelve Steps and Twelve Traditions* (New York: Alcoholics Anonymous World Services, Inc., 2012), 8, emphasis mine.

we'd like to make known, preferably loudly and repeatedly. How else will God know what's best for us unless we tell Him, amen? Nope. We addicts need a narrow lane when it comes to prayer, because having lots of options is precisely the sort of thing that gets us into trouble.

Besides, praying only for knowledge of God's will doesn't have to be scary or painful. If we've repeatedly experienced our addiction's negative consequences, we already know that our self-will is dangerous. Chloe, a recovering sex and love addict, says that doing God's will in one area of her life—like driving on the freeway—makes every area of her life better.

> Driving on the freeway tests my spirituality like nothing else. God's will is for me to be kind to people because we're all deserving of love. But when someone cuts me off, I want to flip them off. I don't want to do God's will in that situation. Scratch that. I *never* want to do God's will. But my self-will fucks things up so badly that God's will is just the better option.[6]

I think Chloe is onto something. And when developing a sober thought life through prayer, I don't have to agonize about finding God's will. It's usually just the next right step. It can be as simple as praying, "Thy will be done, God."

Maybe your sober thought life begins by asking God for the power to wash another load of dirty laundry. Or the power not to be a jerk on the freeway. Maybe you align your

---

6. From a talk given on January 25, 2015, used with permission.

thoughts to God's will by taking your mother's phone call, be-cause she's been trying to call you for weeks and, no, texting doesn't count.

Just as a sober thought life begins with prayer, sober prayer begins with aligning ourselves with God's ideas and plans.

Making Peace with Mystery

In my conversations with other RAs and people who have struggled to build a healthier spirituality, I've heard some helpful stories. Sandra reports that for her, a healthier thought life means being content to understand less:

> I am now insistent that only mystery is certain. There is always more to know, but for all that is known, there is far more that can't be known. It is the very uncertainty that comforts me. In fundamentalism, "faith" meant certainty in the true doctrines and never doubting. "Mystery" was the copout [used] when authorities wanted to shut down questions. In my theology now, faith doubts [and] questions; I am ever seeking. "Mystery" is the acknowledgment that spiritual reality is far too infinite to be confined in doctrines that fit into any words.[7]

Larissa shared that she is now quite comfortable with not having all the right answers: "I actually find it incredibly comforting that there are things that can't be answered because

---

7. Sandra. "Survey Questionnaire for Spiritual Sobriety." E-mail interview by author. April 25, 2015.

they can't possibly be known by humankind. It makes me feel a little less like I need to control everything."[8]

Brenda explained that she can finally admit doubts and feelings of discomfort: "I embrace mystery now. I revel in the confidence to say 'I don't know.' Letting go of certainty makes it easier for me to trust that God is good . . . that God has answers and plans that are better than any idea we could come up with."[9]

Darrell, a non-RA but a man reconstructing his faith, said he was "gradually coming to believe in an entirely different God than I used to. Now I feel I know very little about what there is to know about the true God, and I'm learning to accept that reality. I no longer believe there are simple answers to complex questions, but I'm still sure that God is somehow good."[10]

Dangerous Daydreams

When we're not proactively directing our thoughts through prayer, some of us quickly slip into obsession, fantasy, and magical thinking. For RAs particularly, the habit of indulging fantasies can become extremely detrimental because it often leads to behaviors that compromise their values.

The fantasy may begin harmlessly enough—like imag-

8. Larissa. "Survey Questionnaire for Spiritual Sobriety." E-mail interview by author. April 25, 2015.

9. Brenda. "Survey Questionnaire for Spiritual Sobriety." E-mail interview by author. April 25, 2015.

10. Kathy Escobar, *Faith Shift: Finding Your Way Forward When Everything You Believe Is Coming Apart* (New York: Convergent Books, 2014), 121.

ining the perfect Christian family, romanticizing the home-schooling lifestyle, or comparing our marriages to the "highlight reels" of the godly marriages we admire. The habit addict may daydream about her high-performing children receiving public awards, affirming her status as a superstar mother.

Again, none of these fantasies is inherently bad. But for those struggling to maintain a sober thought life, these innocent daydreams are actually dangerous. They exacerbate restlessness and discontentment—a state of being that triggers acting out in our addiction.

Recovery texts describe the danger of using fantasy to avoid dealing with the real problems of our lives. It's understandable to seek relief when we're feeling stressed, inadequate, or lonely. But using fantasy is injurious to the addict because it allows him or her to numb the pain of seeking sobriety. And that creates more problems.

One such problem is resentment. Because fantasy can alter our perception of reality—for example, seeing a favorite pastor through rose-colored glasses—it's easy to build unrealistic expectations around that person. But what happens when we discover our pastor is really just a flawed human being prone to mistakes? Resentment can easily flare up and destroy the relationship. So much heartache could be avoided if we did not indulge wishful daydreams.

In the late stages of fantasy addiction, we become unable to perform the daily tasks of life. Our habit of dissociation will begin affecting our ability to be present in our families, work, and social relationships.

This is why curbing fantasy is so important for those of

us seeking a sober thought life. Daydreaming can become another addiction. Fantasy creates a narrative at odds with reality. Fantasy never solves our problems but rather makes them worse, because we end up losing time to undisciplined thoughts. Indulging obsession is like being divided against oneself. There's no health in that.

How to Stop

So, how does one cease fantasizing, engaging in magical thinking, and obsessing? We start by learning to catch ourselves when we begin dissociating from the present moment. Again, this takes practice. Be gentle with yourself. Fantasy is a difficult habit to undo. In the beginning, I didn't realize I was fantasizing until I'd already built an entire world complete with characters, dialogue, and costumes! It doesn't matter how often you become aware of addictive thinking as long as you start catching yourself.

Second, we bring ourselves back to the present moment. Some find it helpful to focus on their breath, count to ten, or say aloud, "I am here now." A therapist encouraged me to look around and take note of three things that were happening right in that moment. By becoming aware of our immediate environment, our brains are slowly able to let go of the fantasy.

Third, we identify what we were feeling right before the unhealthy thoughts began. Maybe we heard about a New! Christian! Diet Plan! and we immediately felt bad about the last diet plan we tried and failed at. Maybe some friends of ours attended a big Christian conference and all their gushing on Facebook has left us feeling as if we missed out on a big revival in our generation! Or maybe we heard sad news about a church collapse.

Whatever it was, we try to identify what we were feeling before we sought relief or escape in fantasy, magical thinking, or obsession. Many of us realize that we were experiencing an unmet need (or maybe just a reminder of it), a disappointment, feeling sad, anxious, or angry. Some of us realize we were simply hungry and feeling grouchy. By identifying what was happening just before we slipped into fantasy, we discover clues about why we began using magical thinking.

Last, we gently detach from the fantasy or obsession and replace it with gratitude. There are several ways to do this. Ask yourself if you're engaging inspired imagination or idle daydreams. Imagination taps into our creativity and helps us come up with innovative solutions and ideas, whereas fantasy generally leaves us feeling dissatisfied, restless, and irritable. In other words, imagination is a tool that helps us change the things we can change while fantasy is a distraction that prevents us from accepting the things we can't change.

It's important to be kind while changing your thought habits. Don't force anything. Don't yank your mind around. And refrain from self-shame. Beating yourself up only makes things worse. I try to keep things light and breezy: "Oh, there I go again!"

I refocus myself by taking contrary action. For RAs, we may find it helpful to do something unrelated to religious behavior. Write a thank-you note. Text a friend telling her what you appreciate about her. Walk the dog. Go for a run.

No matter which method you use, by replacing fantasy with contrary action, you give your brain a chance to realign your thoughts with reality—and living in reality is always better for your spiritual sobriety than living in fantasy, magical thinking, or obsession.

Dealing with Shame

Another area in which RAs need help with their thoughts is shame. Many RAs employ the language of shame to chastise themselves. Besides the pain we inflict, feeling self-condemnation leads us to put down others because it's the only way to make ourselves feel morally superior and righteous.

The problem, of course, is that shaming people—including ourselves—doesn't deter us from making mistakes; it only makes us feel worse about them. And then the only way to feel better is to act out our addictive behaviors again. It's a vicious cycle.

Shame tells us we are lovable only when we are performing well. Admitting a mistake means admitting we aren't worthy of love. As it relates to our religious addiction, we may believe our salvation and good standing with God are jeopardized by our mistakes.

One RA I know first heard harsh, condemning words from other Christians. Growing up in a strict religious family, he found his whole perspective shaped by the belief that humans are bad and the world is bad, too. Anything outside his group was suspect, and anything inside his heart was desperately wicked. He was trained to look for failures and mistakes in himself and others. The thing is, when a person grows up this way, his harshest critic is himself.

But if our mistakes are strong enough to compromise God's acceptance of us, isn't that the same as saying our mistakes are stronger than God? This is similar to believing we are born inherently evil. If that were true, then it would mean God created depravity. But just as it is impossible for God to create evil, so it is impossible that our mistakes are stronger than God's hold on us. As Richard Rohr writes, "You are being held so strongly and so deeply that you can stop holding onto, or defending, yourself. God forever sees and loves Christ in you; it is only *we* who doubt our divine identity as children of God. . . . To be fully conscious would be to *love everything* on some level and in some way—even our mistakes."[11]

You wouldn't know it from meeting her, but Tessa, a college student with an easygoing, bohemian style, is a recovering addict who has struggled with shame. "When I find myself saying 'I am a bad person,' that means I'm internalizing my mistakes," she says. "I have to remind myself to stop the Shame Brain!"

Shame Brain happens when we see our mistakes as our identity. It's the difference between "I made an error" and "I am an error." Shame Brain can also take root when we allow others to blame us for things that are not our responsibility—e.g., the way they feel, the mistakes they've made, and so

11. Richard Rohr, *Breathing Under Water: Spirituality and the Twelve Steps* (Cincinnati, OH: Franciscan Media, 2011), 90, 91.

on. Sober thinking means we take responsibility for our own thoughts, feelings, and behaviors while also refraining from taking responsibility for other people's thoughts, feelings, and behaviors.

We are not required to babysit other people's feelings. We don't have to run around checking in with people to make sure they have a favorable opinion of us. If others are mad at us, let them be mad. If people want to leave our lives, we can let them go. It won't kill us (even if it sometimes feels that way). We don't have to know why other people do what they do. Their behaviors don't have to make sense to us. Ultimately, using sober thinking each day helps us be forgiving of ourselves (and others) when we inevitably make mistakes.

When we are living in Shame Brain, little blunders can easily derail our lives. But once we begin the new habit—an act of sober thinking—of embracing our mistakes, we will simply accept them as a normal part of the ups and downs everyone experiences. When we make a mistake, we can acknowledge it and move on. There's no need to beat ourselves up and obsess.

When we know who we really are—loved, loving, and lovable—our mistakes no longer have the power to crush us. And as we honor ourselves by refraining from Shame Brain and thinking sober thoughts, the clarity we seek will be revealed. We will begin to realize our worthiness is not dependent upon what others think of us, say about us, or even upon whether they stay or leave. We will discover that we, like everyone else, are worthy of love and reciprocity in relationships, in our jobs, and in our churches.

The best news of all is that since spiritual sobriety springs from our thoughts, we are not helpless religious addicts; we can change our lives by learning new thought patterns. As we say daily affirmations, offer short, simple prayers, and practice staying present in the moment, we will discover a new way of life emerging: a life free from shame in which we are free to love ourselves and others.

Practice Your Spiritual Sobriety

Prayer:

God, grant me the willingness to let go of thoughts that no longer serve me, and the courage to embrace spiritually sober patterns of thinking.

Promise:

"The Lord is near to those who have a broken heart, and saves such as have a contrite spirit." Psalm 34:18, NKJV

Journaling/Group Questions:

- What recurring thoughts are you ready to let go of? What pattern of thinking are you sick of repeating?
- What negative thoughts can you identify that no longer serve you? Which new, positive thoughts would you like to invite into your mind?
- What three things are you grateful for in your life right now?
- What are three good things about yourself?
- Shame tells us we are lovable only when we're performing well. Describe how performance-driven acceptance has manifested in your life.
- Have you ever experienced Shame Brain? What happens when Shame Brain takes over? Create a simple action plan to help defuse

this issue: 1. Name a person you can call. 2. Choose a self-care exercise. 3. Take contrary action: take a walk, bake cookies, read a book, watch a movie, do something you enjoy.

- Will you commit to replacing unhealthy thoughts? Write down three affirmations you'll say daily.

5

Tame the Wildfire

The Discipline of Kind Speech

Gracious words are a honeycomb, sweet to the soul and healing to the bones.

PROVERBS 16:24, NIV

IN 2013, JUSTINE SACCO WAS THE SENIOR COMMUNICATIONS director of an American media and Internet company. Before a flight to South Africa, Justine tweeted a joke that would forever alter her life: "Going to Africa. Hope I don't get AIDS. Just kidding. I'm white!"

By the time her plane landed in South Africa, the Internet had erupted in collective anger, her employer had publicly condemned the joke, and a Twitter hashtag was trending worldwide: #HasJustineLandedYet. Until she turned on her phone, though, Justine had no idea her thoughtless words had ignited such a wildfire.

She was quickly fired from her job—a decision that even fellow employees at her company believed was necessary. But something else happened, too. As Jon Ronson would later write in the *New York Times*:

> The furor over Sacco's tweet had become not just an ideological crusade against her perceived bigotry but

also a form of idle entertainment. . . . Social media is so perfectly designed to manipulate our desire for approval, and that is what led to her undoing. Her tormentors were instantly congratulated as they took Sacco down, bit by bit, and so they continued to do so. Their motivation was much the same as Sacco's own—a bid for the attention of strangers.[1]

What happened to Justine Sacco is symbolic of a new kind of shaming. These days we don't need pillories or whipping posts. Social media is the only arena we need for public humiliation. You don't even have to do something obviously offensive to receive an avalanche of spite. All you have to do is express an unpopular opinion. Or just be your true, open, vulnerable self.

For religious addicts, kind speech—giving and receiving it—is vital to our healing. Respectful communication (which is sourced, of course, in respectful thinking) helps us build healthy relationships with others and ourselves. Sarcasm, personal attacks, and judgmental comments spring from rage—which is itself a combination of anger and helplessness. But as most of us have discovered, indulging in unkind speech rarely achieves the desired result: namely, changing other people's hearts and minds. Rather, harsh speech makes us become what we hate.

I learned this lesson the hard way. I call it my very own

1. Jon Ronson, "How One Stupid Tweet Blew Up Justine Sacco's Life," *New York Times*, February 14, 2015. Accessed March 30, 2015.

Justine Sacco moment. Except mine didn't happen on Twitter. It happened on national TV in front of millions of viewers.

Verbal Train Wreck

Beginning in 2010, I provided opinion and commentary to Fox News as one of their go-to Mommy bloggers. A producer would e-mail me a link to a recent article or current event and ask for talking points. If my position matched a perspective they wanted represented on the show, they booked me. I was never paid for my appearances. I just did it for fun—and "exposure."

In February 2014, a producer e-mailed me a story about public schools requiring children to bring Valentine's Day cards not just for their friends but for everyone in the class. The producer asked me to supply talking points answering whether the school's policy was really about avoiding hurt feelings or just another case of political correctness run amok.

I replied that I didn't think it was the school's business to tell parents how to celebrate a holiday and that, while the intention was good, children should also be allowed to bring in personalized cards for their closest friends. The producer booked me immediately. The next morning a car picked me up at 3:15 a.m. and drove me to a TV studio in Los Angeles. I stared groggily into the mirror while a makeup artist fixed up my face and hair. Then it was time to get mic'd up and settle in for my "live hit." In my earpiece, I heard the commercial break come to an end.

Elisabeth Hasselbeck introduced the segment by asking

me, "Is it such a bad thing if every child gets a Valentine's Day card, Elizabeth?"

Wait. *What?*

My talking points were focused on the unfairness of banning personalized greetings, not on whether it was a "bad thing" for every child to get a card.

I panicked.

I should have said what I really believed: *Of course everyone should get a card! And children should also be allowed to personalize special cards for their closest friends!* But instead, what came out of my mouth was a confusing tangent about children needing to learn that life isn't fair and nobody wants a generic Valentine's Day card because that's like getting a "pity Valentine" and *Oh my gosh what am I saying?* It was a train wreck. In the end, I sounded like a heartless crone who totally supported excluding kids.

While I was on live TV, I was just scrambling. The segment whizzed by, and I left the studio thinking, *What just happened?* I arrived home feeling sick to my stomach. When I watched the segment I wondered, *Who is that person? And why won't she stop talking?*

Later that day, RawStory.com wrote an article about the segment and hundreds of comments poured in. People called me a whore, a c**t, bat-shit crazy, a bad mother. Another website dubbed me "Asshole of the Day." Then strangers found me on Twitter and started tweeting me directly. It was an avalanche of shame.

I didn't reply or try to defend myself. I knew I'd misspoken. I also knew there was no point trying to explain how I'd misunderstood the premise of the conversation and then panicked on live TV. Either way, it was my fault for not following up with the producer to make sure I understood the focus of the topic and also my fault for saying a bunch of stuff I didn't really believe.

Furthermore, it *was* Fox News. By stepping into that media forum, I'd participated in what they do best: shock and shame. What did I expect? I felt as if I deserved the online beating I received.

A few hours later, though, my e-mail in-box was so full of hate, I felt afraid. I e-mailed the producer and told her about the article at RawStory.com and the e-mails I was getting. She replied curtly that I should just ignore it.

Easy for her to say.

I called one of my friends. Jane listened quietly and then said, "You stated an opinion. But it's just an opinion. It's not who you are. And other people's opinions of you are none of your business. Elizabeth, I mean this: do *not* read any more comments. Maybe shut off the computer and go for a walk."

So I did.

That incident was a huge milestone in my spiritual sobriety. The aftermath of that mistake shook me up so badly that I determined to learn from it, not repeat it. That was the day I realized thoughtless words were not congruent with a sober life. That was the day I committed to break one bad habit: unkind speech.

Gluten- and Humility-Free

During the Recession, I supplemented our family's income by working as a server in a restaurant. One night, an uncomfortable conversation with a customer reminded me of a basic truth I've learned in my religious recovery: no matter how "right" the message, a harsh delivery is always hurtful. In other words, *how* we say things matters.

It was a slow night, and one of my coworkers whipped up some off-the-menu French fries. Later, he offered the fries to one of his regular customers. The guy refused to eat them, saying that he never ate food cooked in the same oil as calamari. I was standing nearby, and he turned to me, pointing a finger at the offending food item. "Those fries have been exposed to flour," he declared. "I'm not sensitive to gluten, but I *choose* to be gluten free!"

I nodded and tried to ignore his disdainful tone. I began clearing a table. But he wasn't done.

"Are *you* gluten free?" he asked.

I was taken aback. "Um, no."

"Well!" He humphed, crossing his arms over his chest. "You should be!"

I chuckled, trying to laugh it off. "Okay. Says who?"

"Says the most amazing doctor anywhere!"

That made me laugh. (The most amazing doctor anywhere, of course, was the man himself.)

"Yes, yes, I am," he continued. "And I'm here to tell you that if you continue eating gluten, you'll develop sensitivity to it. And within five years of continued exposure you go autoimmune. Do you know what that means?"

"Not really."

"It means you're—" He made a cutthroat gesture, accompanied by profanity.

"Huh," I said and reached for the dirty appetizer plates on his table. I was done with this charming exchange.

"He's right, you know," his wife piped up. "He's done a lot of research."

"What kind of doctor did you say you were?" I asked.

"An anti-aging doctor."

"Oh, so a chiropractor then?"

"Well! I've done sixteen years of research!"

I guess my facial expression told him I wasn't buying it, so he turned to his wife. "These are the naysayers, see?"

His wife shook her head, baffled that anyone could doubt him. She gave me a pitying look. "You should listen to him. For your own good."

It's not as if I thought the most amazing doctor anywhere was wrong about gluten. He probably had a point about wheat not being real wheat anymore, what with all the genetic engineering that goes on. But his prideful posture and condescending attitude repelled me from listening. It was the same kind of posturing I remembered from preachers in my fundamentalist church. The topic was different, of course, but the aggressive, judgmental tactic was the same.

Righteous Rhetoric

Driven by fear, the religious addict feels responsible for the eternal salvation of every soul. Different beliefs must be confronted (and eradicated!) because they signal a hellish trajectory. In the pursuit of saving the world, the RA behaves as if the ends justify the means. Judgmental rhetoric is a small price to pay for snatching sinners from the fires of Hell, amen?

In the last twenty-five years, the loudest Christian voices have used their influence to stoke the flames of the so-called culture war. The RA's litmus test for evaluating the damnability of people's souls is whether or not they support same-sex marriage. And during election season, you just might hear a religious addict preach that serving Almighty God means protecting the almighty tax write-offs.

It's understandable why some of us see the church as a splintered, schizophrenic smorgasbord of pet ideologies all competing under the fiercely individualistic ethos of a capitalistic society. No wonder so many churches directly enable religious addicts! They have a tax-exempt status to protect.

But I have to admit my own culpability in using harsh religious rhetoric. I'm quite guilty of it, too.

When I was a new blogger, I was too afraid to tell the stories of spiritual abuse that helped me become a religious addict. It was easier to criticize other bloggers who reminded me of my abusers. It was easier to argue with them in their comment boxes than ask myself why I was having such a strong reaction to their words. There was one woman in particular with whom I disagreed about everything. I couldn't stop reading her blog posts. I was obsessed with how wrong she was, and every time she published some new outrageous content, I was ready to pounce.

Eventually, my constant state of angst and defensiveness leaked into my own writing. I wasn't producing original content as much as I was reacting to everyone else's content. I was incensed over this! Outraged over that! But it all caught up to me when I dashed off a sarcastic blog post about why private Christian schools created little hypocrites. I was reacting to another post I'd read that extolled the virtues of a private Christian education, and since my experience was different, I blasted out an opinion piece. I didn't really think about how the post might affect some of my real-life friends because I was aiming my critique at a blogger I didn't know. But I should have thought about this because someone I knew read the post. And her kids were enrolled in a private Christian school.

Being a gracious and polite woman, my friend didn't confront me about what I'd written, but I noticed a growing distance in our friendship. I finally asked what was wrong, and she told me how my words had hurt her. I tried to reassure her that my post wasn't about her kids, but the damage had already been done. It took some time for me to mend that friendship. A less gracious friend wouldn't have given me a second chance.

Why do we think being sarcastic, online or anywhere, is okay? Why do we say things on social media that we would never say to someone if she were standing in front of us? In our digital age, it feels as if we're losing the skill of polite conversation. Confrontational, indirect, sarcastic communication hurts our relationships—not to mention our sobriety. Hey, few things are more awkward than showing up to a party and realizing you've picked a fight online with at least three people in the room. This has happened to me more than once, and it's always mortifying.

Sarcasm may get page views and retweets on the Internet (which we can easily think means approval), but it also hurts people. The word *sarcasm* comes from the Greek word *sarkasmos*, which is taken from a term meaning "to tear flesh, to bite the lip in rage, sneer."[2] Isn't that what a cutting remark feels like—a tear at the heart?

Sarcasm has the terrible power to ruin relationships. Yet we use it because we like feeling morally or intellectually superior to others. As Alan Turing (played by Benedict Cumberbatch) asks in the movie *The Imitation Game*, "Why do we like violence? Because it feels good." And the anonymity of the Internet makes it easy for us to attack people.

Fasting from Texting

So, how do we attempt to practice spiritual sobriety by building healthy, honest relationships if all the words we use are unkind? Sometimes it might mean fasting—from the Internet, from text messaging, or from whatever communication medium causes us trouble.

My friend Lena, a recovering addict, took a whole year off from text messaging. She said the indirect and reductive nature of that activity was hindering her ability to build true, authentic friendships. At her sponsor's suggestion, Lena forced herself to make phone calls instead. At first, this was very awkward.

"When people asked for my phone number, I'd have to tell them that I didn't text, and they'd look at me like I was crazy,"

2. "Sarcasm." *Wikipedia*. Accessed April 1, 2015. http://en.wikipedia.org/wiki /Sarcasm#cite_note-OED-1.

Lena says. "But then I realized that if someone was truly interested in having a relationship with me, they'd make the effort to call. I had to get over my own reluctance and make calls, too. Turned out making phone calls and having direct contact with people really helped my sobriety."

Lena makes a great point. Direct contact, by its very nature, discourages inappropriate speech. As long as we are texting, instant messaging, or e-mailing people, we are always at least two steps removed. We can listen passively and respond whenever we want—or not.

When instead we engage others directly, we practice important interpersonal skills like listening. As we develop good listening skills, our speech will become less hasty and, therefore, less hurtful because we will have learned to listen to the feelings underneath the words. This is called "empathic listening," and according to Christine M. Riordan, provost and professor of management at University of Kentucky, this activity is very helpful in relationships: "Among its benefits, empathic listening builds trust and respect, enables people to reveal their emotions—including tensions, facilitates openness of information sharing, and creates an environment that encourages collaborative problem-solving."[3]

Direct communication and empathic listening are indispensable tools for building healthy, sober communication.

3. Christine M. Riordan, "Three Ways Leaders Can Listen with More Empathy," *Harvard Business Review*, January 16, 2014. Accessed April 2, 2015. https://hbr .org/2014/01/three-ways-leaders-can-listen-with-more-empathy.

Honest but Not Mean

My career as an online writer almost demands that I make a habit of using colorful, provocative language. The splashier and more controversial your blog, the more attention you'll get. I've justified harsh posts by saying things like: "Well, sometimes the truth hurts" or "Hey, I'm just being honest!"

I've learned the hard way (through damaged friendships) that "just being honest" isn't an excuse for being unkind. I'm guilty of saying things online that I would never say face-to-face. When someone writes or says something I don't agree with and I experience a surge of panic, as an RA seeking sobriety I try not to react immediately. This gives me the space I need to reflect on why that person's opinions bother me so much, which often leads me to discover that my strong reaction is sourced in my own fears and insecurities. Growing up in a religiously addicted environment, I believed conformity of belief was vital to my survival. But now that I am free and pursuing sobriety, differing opinions and beliefs are no longer a threat. Instead of reacting negatively to others' opinions (or to difficult people!), the spiritually sober person can take time for self-reflection and then search for common ground.

Words have a tremendous power to hurt people, but they also have the life-changing power to heal and edify. One way we can do this is by keeping the focus on ourselves. Therapists and counselors often advise their clients to use "I" statements instead of "you" statements. For example, "I feel uncomfortable" instead of "You make me uncomfortable." It's a small change, but it can dissolve the tension in a conversation and open the possibility for constructive dialogue.

There are other ways we can use our words positively. In support groups, for example, members are encouraged to avoid "cross talk" and not repeat the stories they hear outside the group. This creates a safe space in which people can share honestly. When we aren't worried about being judged, we tell the stories we've been too afraid to share elsewhere. When we know our information won't be gossiped to others, we can be vulnerable enough to display our feelings. The virtuous cycle of understanding begins when we each speak honestly and vulnerably, thereby making it safe for others to do so as well.

We can employ the tools of safe sharing not only in support groups, but in all our relationships. When someone else is brave enough to be vulnerable with us, we can honor his or her courage by not judging or giving advice. Other people's mistakes are not our opportunities to shame them, goad them for an explanation, broadcast their hypocrisy, or compare them to other people who have failed.

We must take special care to respect others' dignity by using our words wisely—even if we think they don't deserve it. Kind speech isn't just good for others; it also benefits *our* dignity and our spiritual sobriety.

Practice Your Spiritual Sobriety

Prayer:

   God, grant me a new inner soundtrack of self-acceptance and love so that the words I speak offer compassion and understanding to others.

Promise:

"Reckless words pierce like a sword, but the tongue of the wise brings healing." Proverbs 12:18, NIV

Journaling/Group Questions:

- Have you ever regretted something you said? Can you remember how horrified you felt after you realized you'd hurt someone's feelings or lashed out in a moment of anger? When developing a habit of kind speech, what sort of guidelines do you think are important? Why?

- Write down three examples of unkind statements you've spoken about yourself. Where did these words come from? Do you believe they are true?

- Have you ever used harsh, sarcastic, or judgmental words in online conversations? What was the result?

- Has someone ever attacked you on the Internet? How did that affect you?

- Have you ever experienced public shaming in church or been the brunt of a pastor's sermon illustration? How did you feel?

- Think of a friend you haven't talked to or seen in a while. Take the time to place a phone call (don't e-mail or text!). A conversation with a friend—or even just leaving an encouraging voice mail—will brighten your day.

- Is someone you know going through a rough time in life? Write a note of encouragement. Using kind words helps others *and* helps us.

6

The Genius of Moderation

How Sobriety Keeps Us from Burnout

> Happiness is when what you think, what you say, and what you do
> are in harmony.
>
> —*MAHATMA GANDHI*

FRANTIC BEHAVIORS AND A PRIDE OF URGENCY ARE THE
natural outcome for someone living inside a high-demand religious environment—and also in our fast-paced, oversched-
uled, modern American society.

Whether we are religious addicts or just your average,
garden-variety workaholics (*aka* habit addicts), we always
push hard. We leave nothing on the table. We go all or nothing *all the time*!

And then we burn out.

Author and researcher Brené Brown says that Americans
often "wear exhaustion as a status symbol." We are motivated
by beliefs that we're inadequate, that we're frauds. We are
judgmental; we base our self-worth on productivity. According to her research, Brown says women are driven to "do it
all, do it perfectly and make sure you make it look effortless."
Men, on the other hand, experience shame when they are
perceived as weak. A husband and father once told Brown

that his family would rather see him "die atop my white horse than have to watch me fall off."[1]

This is no way to live.

And yet, how do we live differently? Soberly?

For many of us addicts, going forward serenely and moderately may feel almost blasphemous. Being "lukewarm" is discouraged in church, but it's also discouraged in the office. We feel pressured to work long hours and not just hit our quotas but exceed them. Whether we're on social media or in the boardroom, we must be always ready with a witty tweet or an impressive answer.

For Christians, being lukewarm is almost as bad as not believing at all. We'd rather burn out for Jesus than take the seemingly lazy road of moderation. A mom named Jenny shared how she missed out on her firstborn's early years because she was so busy:

> I spent my twenties planting a church. I had my infant son sleep under desks so I could work at the church office. He's nineteen now but I still have such deep grief. It wasn't until I gave birth to my second son, suffered postpartum depression, and dragged myself into my doctor's office that I began to see [what was happening to me]. I've been on meds ever since.[2]

1. Krista Tippett, "Brené Brown: The Courage to Be Vulnerable." On Being. January 25, 2015. Accessed March 17, 2015. http://www.onbeing.org/program/brene-brown-on-vulnerability/4928.

2. "Have You Experienced 'Burning Out' for Jesus?" Online interview by author. April 26, 2015.

For RAs, living moderately may be scary because we believe that working hard is the only way to guarantee approval from God and meaning in our lives. Likewise, habit addicts may feel averse to moderation because it means giving up perfectionism, workaholism, or other compulsive behaviors that help us feel in control of life. But our resistance to moderation is more a reflection of our performance-driven society than a reflection of our value or God's heart toward us. While good works are evidence of fervent faith, they have nothing to do with our status as people before God. God's love for us just *is*. God's love for us is our preexisting condition. We are not inherently evil; we are inherently loved.

This doesn't mean we sit around and do nothing, of course. It just means we learn to live thoughtfully, soberly—*moderately*. In her research, Brené Brown found that people who allowed themselves to be vulnerable even when there was no guarantee of success were the ones living courageously and wholeheartedly.[3] If we can learn to try a saner way of living, we may just find ourselves on the path to a better life.

Take It Easy

When we set out to build a new, sober life, we must begin gently. For many of us, this means not trying to work on everything at once. Our tendency as addicts is to attack all the problems in one fell swoop. But this ends in exhaustion and frustration. Daily consistency is far more effective than inconsistent bursts of action.

3. Tippett, "Brené Brown."

Rather than attempt a complete overhaul of our lives, we better serve our spiritual sobriety by taking things slowly, one day at a time. Do small things well. Be content with the completion of each day's necessary tasks without overdoing it. God will show up in our lives in unexpected ways without our having to try so hard.

Describing how she learned to relax in her spiritual journey, a woman named Rachel wrote:

I was killing myself [like any good addict] trying to have a meaningful God experience: I got up an hour early for devotions, then two hours earlier for *more* devotions. Finally, someone told me to just stop doing everything for a while because I couldn't force God to speak to me. He'd find me when He had something to say. So I stopped guilting myself. And God started showing up in songs or books or as I was walking or shopping. I've given up on the perfect devotional life and find myself much happier and calmer in my faith.[4]

This was also Osanna's experience when she sought sobriety.

I stopped every religious practice I had done. No church, Bible reading, Bible study, worship music, or prayer. And God found me. He found me on a walk, on a hike, on a run. He found me when the sorrow of my heart was so

---

4. "Have You Experienced 'Burning Out' for Jesus?" Online interview by author. April 26, 2015.

powerful I could not stand. He found me in conversations with friends. He found me. And he met me in my deepest brokenness. And then he restored my soul. He gave me a new hope and a joyful song.[5]

Pastor and author Nadia Bolz-Weber writes about the downtime God wants us to savor:

Sacred rest is a break from the am-I-productive-enough, lovable enough, safe enough, thin enough, rich enough, strong enough-worthiness system we live under. The sacred rest that is yours never comes from being worthy. It never comes through adopting the right kind and the right amount and the right quality of spiritual practices. . . . [T]he rest that is yours and mine comes from the promise of the Gospel: that Jesus came to save sinners, that Jesus came to heal and love and save the sin-sick and the over-functioning, that Jesus came to give rest to the weary, and the restless. . . .

So rest. Rest knowing that you are justified, not by your busyness, but by grace through faith. Rest in the knowledge of how madly God loves you. Not because of who you are, but because of who God is. Rest in that. Not because you should. But because you can.[6]

5. Osanna. "Survey Questionnaire for Spiritual Sobriety." E-mail interview by author. April 25, 2015.

6. Nadia Bolz-Weber, blogpost: "A Sermon on No Time to Rest and Also No Jetpacks." July 20, 2015. http://www.patheos.com/blogs/nadiabolzweber/2015/07/a-sermon-on-no-time-to-rest-and-also-no-jetpacks/.

In recommending how to begin this journey, St. Francis de Sales suggests a tranquil, methodical approach to our daily tasks.

> Be careful and diligent in all your affairs . . . give them your best attention. Do not set about your work with restlessness and excitement, and do not give way to bustle and eagerness in what you do; every form of excitement affects both judgment and reason, and hinders a right performance of the very thing which excites us. . . . If you attempt to do everything at once, or with confusion . . . you will probably be overwhelmed and accomplish nothing.[7]

St. Francis isn't saying that working enthusiastically is wrong; he's saying that it's better to perform our tasks in "quiet cooperation with [God]"[8] than to rely on high-intensity feelings.

If we consistently focus on simply performing our daily tasks, the whole-life transformation we desire will begin to happen naturally. It won't occur overnight, and we may not always see our progress. But as a woman named Allis wrote on my Facebook page: "*Very* slowly I am finding healing, both mentally and spiritually. I am spending more time on the Path and less time in the ditches."[9]

We don't have to stress out about being lukewarm or

7. St. Francis de Sales, *Introduction to the Devout Life* (New York: Random House, 2002), 114.

8. Ibid.

9. "Have You Experienced 'Burning Out' for Jesus?" Online interview by author. April 26, 2015.

worry that we're not doing enough. God will find us when He has something to say.

Self-Care Isn't Selfish

Often we RAs assume it's somehow holier to give from a place of scarcity. Perhaps we were taught that generosity meant giving more than we had and that "good Christians" always said yes whenever they were asked for help. We were taught to share at the expense of our own well-being. We came to associate self-care and self-love with selfishness.

Harmful giving happens when we compulsively take care of others' needs while neglecting our own. In order to feed others, we ourselves must be fed. Reflexively taking care of others while neglecting our own needs damages our ability to live the sober life we crave. I've heard recovering codependents say they were so busy being present in other people's lives that they weren't present in their own. If we can't feel good unless others behave the way we want them to, we're not actually helping them; we're meddling. And meddling isn't helpful to others—it's a compulsion that feeds our unhealthy need for control.

But supplying help from a position of scarcity doesn't help others as much as if we supply from a position of abundance. Author and pastor Kathy Escobar explains how viewing self-care as self-centeredness actually inhibits us from loving others well.

Many of us were taught that loving ourselves or saying no to others' requests was a sin of self-centeredness. In reality, it is foundational to loving our neighbors properly. Because so many of us have grown up in our faith feeling insecure, unworthy, and unlovable in God's eyes, we love our neighbor from that broken place instead of a secure, free one. It's also why a lot of us are horrible at taking care of ourselves. We've been led to believe that everything in our lives should be about God and others. We've sadly missed the point that our ability to love God and others comes from how we love ourselves.[10]

Religious addicts are especially prone to self-neglect because Scripture texts are frequently misinterpreted to equate self-hatred with godliness. Calvinistic doctrines like "total depravity" reinforce self-loathing. God intended for us to need Him because the beautiful plans He has for us find their fulfillment in communion with Him—not because we're bad.

When we neglect ourselves, long-term stress takes a toll on our bodies, sometimes leading to chronic, stress-related illnesses. If we make compulsive caretaking of others a lifestyle, we can become so absent from ourselves that we lose the ability to identify what we're feeling and what we need—not to mention what we want. Eventually, we may neglect even basic self-care like proper nutrition, dental hygiene, and rest. Just as doctors tell us preventive health care is less expensive than treatment for disease, so self-care is less expensive to us emotionally, physically, and spiritually than treatment for burnout.

10. Kathy Escobar, *Faith Shift: Finding Your Way Forward When Everything You Believe Is Coming Apart* (New York: Convergent Books, 2014), 83.

Ari writes, "I have had to learn and relearn who I am and respect that, to respect my needs and opinions [and] my viewpoint. I have had to learn how to be gentle with myself, care for myself, and trust the healthy voice inside my head. . . . This is very much a work in progress."[11]

Author and blogger Micha Boyett writes that motherhood is the place where she recognizes the importance of slowing down and living life at her children's pace. "I am addicted to my own franticness," she writes. "I am addicted to performing enough, in the right amount of time, in a way that the people around me say is good."[12]

We, too, may find that we are addicted to franticness. In fact, isn't that really the core of our acting-out behaviors—a need to control? As we continue our spiritual sobriety journey, we may even find a tendency to overwork our recovery. When I first started attending twelve-step programs, I was so excited about what I'd found that I threw myself into working the steps, reading all the literature, attending all the meetings.

One day, my sponsor showed up to a meeting with a little medallion for me. I was thrilled. Ooooh! A miniature trophy to celebrate all the hard work I was doing? She chuckled as she handed it to me, saying, "I thought you might need this." I turned the medallion over in my hand: *Keep It Sim-*

11. Ari. "Survey Questionnaire for Spiritual Sobriety." E-mail interview by author. April 25, 2015.

12. Micha Boyett. "Recovery Room: The Internal Frantic Monster (Or, My Addiction to the Egg Timer)." SethHaines.com "The Recovery Room." March 26, 2015. http://sethhaines.com/addiction/recovery-room-the-internal-frantic-monster-or-my -addiction-to-the-egg-timer/.

ple. What? No kudos for my frenzied recovery performance? Nope. Just *Keep It Simple*. I really should have taken that advice. But I didn't. I was convinced—like most addicts!— that trying harder and working harder would produce more results. In other words, I didn't pace myself.

Destructive Extremes

In most twelve-step programs, addicts are advised to attend at least three meetings a week—if not one meeting per day. But for a religious addict like me, already prone to overworking, that advice can backfire. As I mentioned, I overdid my attempts at recovery. I attended three to five twelve-step meetings a week (Co-Dependents Anonymous, Love & Sex Addicts Anonymous, and Al-Anon), made daily outreach calls, and spent too much time making sure I had done all of my "step work." When I found myself falling down the rabbit hole of self-loathing or burnout, the advice I frequently received was just to attend more meetings, make more calls, do more step work, and that it would work if I stayed with it.

One day it struck me that some of the twelve-step groups I was attending functioned very similarly to the childhood cult I was raised in. I could see how a very structured, hard-working mentality would be quite helpful to an addict who was raised *without* structure, rules, schedules, and accountability partners. But since I'd been raised with too much rigidity, my intense twelve-step program was beginning to harm my recovery. I had to realize I had the freedom and permission to build a recovery routine that fit *me*, not force myself to squeeze into a program that worked for others. Once again, it was about learning to live moderately—even in my recovery. (More on this in chapter 9.)

For me, the solution wasn't to stop attending twelve-step meetings altogether. I just dialed back my attendance a little bit. One or two meetings a week was more than enough. The rest of the week, I needed to prioritize rest and self-care.

Essentially, a healthy, affirming recovery helps us avoid extremes. Some of us tend either to neglect everything in order to take care of ourselves or to neglect ourselves in order to take care of others. But spiritual sobriety is most effective when we establish simple, daily routines that incorporate times of rest, recreation, and work. Whenever we find ourselves slipping into extremes, we need to realize we're headed toward an unstable state that could compromise our spiritual sobriety.

That state may look like black-and-white thinking, catastrophic forecasts of the future, attacking tasks with a vengeance, trying to change things that are entirely out of our control, staying up too late because we need to get more done, not exercising (or overexercising), starving ourselves, overeating, not letting ourselves reach out for help, not talking about what we're going through, and paranoia.

For some addicts, when they feel strung out, obsessive, or irritable it is helpful for them to slow down and ask themselves if they are feeling hungry, angry, lonely, or tired.[13] If so, then they should attend to that need instead of plowing ahead with whatever else seems more urgent. The more they

13. Samantha Lauria, "H.A.L.T.," Addiction-recovery.com, http://www.addiction
-recovery.com/HALT-hungry-angry-lonely-tired.php. Accessed January 5, 2016.

do this, the more they realize how often they override their legitimate needs.

So much of our anger, frustration, and difficulty could be avoided if we simply went to bed when we were tired, ate when we were hungry, and called a friend when we were angry or lonely. Frankly, addicts expend a lot of energy on not feeling their needs. RAs feel guilty for being human. We believe others are worthy of having their needs met but we aren't.

Once we start accepting that our needs aren't bad—indeed, God created us with them!—we stop feeling guilty for practicing self-care. In the words of a daily devotional, "Maybe Someone gave me the need because Someone planned to fulfill it. Maybe I had to feel the need, so I would notice and accept the gift."[14]

Get Bored and Banish Burnout

For addicts, ordinary life feels dull. We need big things to be always happening. We aren't just addicted to the highs; we are also probably addicted to the lows. If we can't get high on church services, dynamic speakers, emotive music, hitting quotas at work, shopping, dieting, browsing the Internet, or any other behavior, we at least want to ramp up the intensity through drama, overcommitting ourselves to projects, or growing defensive about our newfound enlightenment. We want anything—*anything* other than what we perceive to be the mundane tasks of ordinary life.

14. Melody Beattie, *The Language of Letting Go* (Center City, MN: Hazelden, 1990), 85.

Ironically, by constantly seeking excitement, we actually prevent ourselves from experiencing the full range of pleasure that ordinary—sober—life has to offer. As philosopher Bertrand Russell wrote: "A life too full of excitement is an exhausting life, in which continually stronger stimuli are needed. . . . Too much excitement not only undermines the health, but dulls the palate for every kind of pleasure. . . . A certain power of enduring boredom is therefore essential to a happy life."[15]

Boredom—inactivity—is essential to a happy life? How is that possible?

Well, for one thing, psychologists have found that boredom enhances creativity. In experiments with children, those who were given a creative project after performing a boring task actually invented more ways of using the materials than the children from the control group. Dr. Sandi Mann, the psychologist leading the study, concluded, "Boredom is a fascinating emotion because it is seen as so negative yet it is such a motivating force."[16]

If boredom is good for creativity and vital for a pleasurable life, we addicts—religious or otherwise—need to start letting ourselves be bored once in a while. This is easier said than done. Many of us hail from church cultures where

15. Quoted in Maria Popova, "In Defense of Boredom: 200 Years of Ideas on the Virtues of Not-Doing from Some of Humanity's Greatest Minds," Brain Pickings RSS, March 16, 2015. Accessed March 17, 2015. http://www.brainpickings .org/2015/03/16/boredom/.

16. Sarah Knapton, "Boredom Makes People More Creative, Claim Psychologists," *The Telegraph*, March 25, 2015. Accessed March 28, 2015. http://www .telegraph.co.uk/news/science/science-news/11492867/Boredom-makes-people -more-creative-claim-psychologists.html.

the depth of our commitment to God was directly linked to the breadth of our commitment to church work. Unless our schedules are jam-packed with church-related activities, work, or recreation, we fear we're missing out on the American Dream or what God is accomplishing in the world. We may be so terrified of our own boredom that we compulsively seek excitement and activity wherever we can. We may even see boredom as sin. No wonder we live on the brink of burnout.

Maybe embracing boredom is exactly the kind of sober action our recovery needs. Boredom is a state of nonaction. Many of us have been so busy doing that there's no time to slow down and let ourselves *be*. Many religious addicts assume that being busy for God is the same as having intimacy with God. It's not. Giving ourselves permission to embrace a state of non-doing can provide time for important breakthroughs.

I try to do this by placing boundaries. For example, you might try one simple rule: no drama after 5 p.m. Part of our patterns as RAs is to manufacture fireworks. We crave them. To counteract this craving, we could stop checking e-mail, engaging in arguments, or making a big deal out of *anything* after five o'clock. Whatever (alleged) crisis arises can always be dealt with the next day. The end of the day is for winding down and relaxing. When we're tired, problems are always overwhelming. When we're rested, conflicts are far more manageable. Placing a boundary around our evenings helps us embrace the necessary boredom/slowness that lends itself to rejuvenating rest.

But let me be honest: it's easy to fail at this. It's really,

really difficult for RAs to chill out and relax anytime! We can get super antsy and annoyed. Embracing boredom takes practice. It means saying no to ourselves. But it keeps burnout at bay.

The Power of No

In an article for the *Harvard Business Review*, bestselling author Greg McKeown wrote that declining opportunities is "not just haphazardly saying no, but purposefully, deliberately, and strategically eliminating the nonessentials. Not just once a year as part of a planning meeting, but constantly reducing, focusing and simplifying. Not just getting rid of the obvious time wasters, but being willing to cut out really terrific opportunities as well."[17]

In her bestselling book, *The Fringe Hours*, Jessica Turner describes the benefits of saying no:

> In the past, I have always been the first to volunteer and say yes to everything. Over time, I have learned that this leads to me being overextended, exhausted and not pleasant to be around. Now I give myself permission to say no, to stick to my decision, and to not feel guilty about it. Moreover, I have learned that while I sometimes regret saying yes, I never regret saying no.[18]

17. Greg McKeown, "The Disciplined Pursuit of Less," *Harvard Business Review*, August 8, 2012. Accessed March 28, 2015. https://hbr.org/2012/08/the-disciplined -pursuit-of-less.

18. Jessica N. Turner, *The Fringe Hours: Making Time for You* (Grand Rapids, MI: Revell, 2015), 142.

Religious and habit addicts often feel terrible guilt for saying no because they may have been taught to see it as a character defect, an inability to commit. Nothing could be further from the truth. As they learn how to say yes in sobriety (by choosing self-care first), they also learn how to say no: purposefully, deliberately, and strategically. Think of no as a muscle that needs daily exercise to stay strong. If you're saying yes to everything, then you're really saying no to self-care. Exercising your no teaches you how to stand up for yourself.

The most successful people say no a lot so that they can say yes to a few very important things. And that is the crux of sober action: saying no to our addictive behaviors so that we are free to say yes to energy-inspiring behaviors and ultimately, yes to happiness. Living moderately creates the space and the energy to make these supremely healthy choices.

Practice Your Spiritual Sobriety

Prayer:
   God, help me slow down and cease from frantic urgency. Help me honor my human needs by prioritizing self-care and the patience to live moderately.

Promise:
   "For my yoke is easy to bear, and the burden I give you is light." Matthew 11:30, NLT

Journaling/Group Questions:
• Have you ever experienced burnout? In what ways were you over-committed? How did this impact your health and well-being? What can you do differently? What specific limits are you willing to place, for

example, on your work hours—i.e., not bringing work home from the office, turning off your computer and cell phone at a certain time, not replying to work-related requests after 7 p.m.? How can you enhance your sobriety by setting limits on your religious activity—e.g., attending one church service on Sunday rather than two or three; reading a short devotional every day rather than a whole chapter of Scripture.

- Have you ever experienced burnout for Jesus? What did that look like for you? What were the physical, emotional, or spiritual effects?
- "God's love for us is our preexisting condition. We are not inherently evil; we are inherently loved." How do these statements sit with you? Are they hard to believe? How would your life change if you believed nothing could change God's love for you?
- List three ways you can take care of yourself today.
- Describe how you will experiment with boredom to see if it enhances creativity or inspires moderation.
- Do you feel guilty for saying no to people? Choose one exercise to perform each day for a week in order to strengthen your no muscle: 1. Eliminate two items from your daily to-do list. 2. Ask for help with a specific task. 3. Delegate a task to someone else. 4. Schedule a massage/nail appointment/social event to look forward to. 5. Look over next month's schedule and plan four downtime days for yourself. 6. Journal about what events and activities make you feel good and be honest about which ones are draining your energy. 7. Talk to a trusted friend about ideas for simplifying your schedule.

7

Unclench

Sobriety in Our Relationships

The ultimate lesson all of us have to learn is unconditional love,
which includes not only others but ourselves as well.

—ELISABETH KÜBLER-ROSS

IN SPIRITUAL SOBRIETY, WE LEARN TO HOLD RELATIONSHIPS
loosely, lightly. We discover that other people are not ours to
manipulate or control—even when we think we know what's
best for them. A spiritually sober person respects the personal
boundaries and inherent dignity of others. By unclenching
our hands, we actually enjoy our relationships more.

Spiritually sober relationships are characterized by trust
and unconditional love. If we're able to enjoy a daily relationship with an unconditionally loving God, it builds our capac-
ity to trust Him, trust ourselves, and trust others—because
we're confident that God, not our friends, will guide us and
provide for our needs.

Our sober relationships with God, self, and others are
achieved by nonpossessive behavior, erecting and respecting
boundaries, and offering and experiencing forgiveness. Practicing these three things helps us maintain balance, dignity,
and realistic expectations in our relationships.

And it all begins with love.

In his book *The Inner Voice of Love*, Henri Nouwen writes, "God has given you a beautiful self. There God dwells and loves you with the first love, which precedes all human love. You carry your own beautiful, deeply loved self in your heart."[1] Learning to love ourselves is loving the way God loves us. Self-rejection and self-loathing are dangerous enemies to spiritual sobriety, because they contradict what God says about us. Learning to love the selves God has made us is a wellspring from which our love for others will grow, too.

We may feel really uncomfortable with the terms *self-forgiveness* and *self-love* because people in many religious circles mock those terms as empty pop-psychology. But this is where licensed professional counselors become indispensable, because before we can have healthy relationships with others, we must first mend our relationship with ourselves. Most of us can't do this alone. A counselor can help us identify events in our lives that hurt us. Understanding our pasts helps us empathize with our current selves—not in a self-pitying way, but in a manner that motivates us to enact positive change.

Loving oneself isn't the emotional equivalent of placing a flattering filter over a photograph on Instagram; it's more like studying an unblemished image of ourselves as cherished children of God. When we see ourselves this way, it's far easier to admit our wrongdoing and forgive ourselves.

Religious addicts often carry burdens of guilt for the ways they've abused themselves and others. As we seek re-

1. Henri J. M. Nouwen, *The Inner Voice of Love: A Journey Through Anguish to Freedom* (New York: Doubleday, 1996), 29.

covery, we may find it helpful to make a list of people we have wronged. Even if we can't make direct amends to those we've hurt (because making contact would reinjure them), being honest about what we've done is an important step in self-forgiveness. Once we've made our list, sharing it with a trusted friend or therapist will relieve us of the shame we've carried and free our hearts to develop a more loving relationship with ourselves—and others.

Modeling Self-Trusting Behavior

Spiritually sober relationships spring from unconditional love and trust. As addicts, we mend our relationships by learning to first trust ourselves. If we've engaged in addictive behavior, religious or otherwise, for a sustained period of time, we've probably lost faith in our ability to conduct our lives in a healthy way.

Those of us RAs who experienced spiritually abusive homes or churches were specifically taught *not* to rely on ourselves. Verses like Proverbs 3:5—"Trust in the Lord with all your heart and lean not on your own understanding"—were used to warn us that trusting ourselves would make us vulnerable prey to Satan. But usually, the people quoting these verses to us weren't teaching us to put faith in the Lord; they were teaching us to trust our church leaders.

Ironically, placing blind trust in other humans is exactly what made us vulnerable prey—not to Satan, but to addiction. These leaders didn't have to earn our trust. We just had to believe in them because, well, they were the leaders.

We learn to distrust ourselves when "we have a feeling and

we're told it's wrong or inappropriate," Melody Beattie writes. "We lose faith in that deep, important part of ourselves that feels appropriate feelings, senses truth, and has confidence in its ability to handle life's situations. Pretty soon, we may believe what we are told about ourselves—that we're off, a tad crazy, not to be trusted."[2]

Cynthia Lynn Wall, author of *The Courage to Trust: A Guide to Building Deep and Lasting Relationships*, affirms, "No one can be as consistently supportive of you as you can learn to be. Being kind to yourself increases self-confidence and lessens your need for approval. Loving and caring for yourself not only increases self-trust, it also deepens your connection with others."[3]

Spiritual sobriety means learning to trust ourselves by refusing to invalidate our thoughts and feelings, ignore our needs, and/or beat ourselves up. If we are to recover trust in our gut instinct and our ability to sense truth, we must practice owning, honoring, and validating our experiences as true and real. We don't have to wait for others to corroborate our experience before we trust what we experience. Other people don't get to tell us our reality; we can learn to trust what we feel and think—and even how we act.

Furthermore, when we model self-trusting behavior, we give others permission to trust themselves, too. Empowerment is contagious. As we own our own thoughts, feelings, and needs, we teach others what healthy, mature, sober be-

2. Melody Beattie, *Codependent No More* (Center City, MN: Hazelden, 1992), 103.

3. Cynthia L. Wall, LCSW, *The Courage to Trust: A Guide to Building Deep and Lasting Relationships* (Oakland, CA: New Harbinger Publications, 2005).

havior looks like. When we believe in ourselves and empower others to do the same, we break self-destructive cycles and create new, life-enhancing cycles.

And yes, learning to trust ourselves might mean making some mistakes in relationships but making mistakes is okay, too. It's how we learn.

The authors of *Take Back Your Life: Recovering from Cults and Abusive Relationships* suggest writing a personal Bill of Rights. Even though this list is primarily directed to survivors of abusive churches and relationships, RAs and habit addicts can benefit from this confidence-building exercise. Here's an example.

- I have the right to evaluate my own behavior, thoughts, and emotions, and to take responsibility for their initiation and consequences upon myself.
- I have the right to decide whether I am responsible for solving other people's problems.
- I have the right to change my mind.
- I have the right to make mistakes—and be responsible for them.
- I have the right to be illogical in making decisions.
- I have the right to say I don't know.
- I have the right to say I don't understand.
- I have the right to say I don't care.
- I have the right to set my own priorities.
- I have the right to say no without feeling guilty.[4]

4. Janja Lalich and Madeleine Tobias, *Take Back Your Life: Recovering from Cults and Abusive Relationships* (Berkeley, CA: Bay Tree Pub., 2006), 155–56.

Writing such a statement helps us remember that not only do we have rights, but others do, too. Knowing what is mine and what is not is an essential prerequisite for spiritually sober relationships.

As Z. Hereford writes, "You are the highest authority on you. You know yourself best. *You* know what you need, want, and value. Don't let anyone make the decisions for you. . . . An unhealthy imbalance occurs when you encourage neediness, or are needy; want to be rescued, or are the rescuer, or when you choose to play the victim."[5]

You Are the Gatekeeper

A way to avoid the imbalance Hereford describes is to create meaningful personal boundaries. Sober relationships are characterized by such smart walls. What am I talking about?

A boundary is a space between you and another person [or belief system or religious community]. Think of it as a fence or a gate. As the gatekeeper, you can decide how close [something or someone] gets to you. . . . Healthy boundaries are a way to protect yourself, giving yourself freedom to conduct your life in a way that helps you flourish.[6]

5. Z. Hereford, "Healthy Boundaries and How to Establish Them." http://www .essentiallifeskills.net/personalboundaries.html. Accessed July 22, 2015.

6. "How to Establish Boundaries," http://liveboldandbloom.com/08/life-coaching /want-to-boost-your-self-esteem-10-ways-to-establish-personal-boundaries#sthash .b6iLc7bA.dpuf. Accessed July 22, 2015.

Another definition:

Personal boundaries are the imaginary lines we draw around ourselves to maintain balance and protect our bodies, minds, emotions, and time from the behavior or demands of others. They provide us the framework to keep us from being used or manipulated by others, and they allow us to confidently express who we are and what we want in life.[7]

Without them, our vulnerabilities become liabilities, and we are often left feeling used and discarded. Our open-heartedness turns into cynicism and resentment. Strong boundaries are important for us addicts, because they protect us from enduring (more) harm.

Religious addicts especially need boundaries, because they tend to live at extremes and suffer the consequences: their spiritual zeal has left them used up and burnt out by others' demands, they are exhausted from too much giving and striving to please, and they are disillusioned by a lack of healthy give-and-take relationships. When we recognize our addiction, we realize there must be a better way. Boundaries are a tool for the better way.

The great news is, once we've made use of this tool, once we erect and maintain strong boundaries, we discover our self-confidence has increased, our communication has

7. Barrie Davenport, "10 Ways to Establish Personal Boundaries," http://live boldandbloom.com/08/life-coaching/want-to-boost-your-self-esteem-10-ways-to -establish-personal-boundaries#sthash.b6iLc7bA.dpuf. Accessed July 22, 2015.

improved, our relationships are more satisfying, and we feel more stable and in control. "You must take responsibility for how you allow others to treat you," says one writer. "Your boundaries act as filters permitting what is acceptable in your life and what is not."[8]

Self-Test: Do You Need Boundaries?

Not sure yet if you *need* emotional fences? See if any of these descriptions sounds familiar:

- Feeling guilty when you . . . say no.
- Acting against your integrity or values in order to please.
- Not speaking up when you have something to say.
- Adopting another person's beliefs or ideas so that you are accepted.
- Not calling out someone who mistreats you.
- Giving too much just to be perceived as useful.
- Becoming overly involved in someone's problems or difficulties.
- Allowing people to say things to you or in front of you that make you uncomfortable.
- Not defining and communicating your emotional needs in your closest relationships.[9]

Adds Barrie Davenport, "When you have weak personal boundaries, every act of compliance, self-denial, or needi-

8. Hereford, "Healthy Boundaries."
9. Davenport, "10 Ways."

ness chips away at your self-respect. . . . You are in a constant state of insecurity."[10]

If developing boundaries seems overwhelming, do it anyway. As one writer says, it's actually "an exciting adventure, an exercise in personal liberation. It means coming to know ourselves and increasing our awareness of what we stand for. It also means self-acceptance and knowing that we are OK as we are and worthy of the good things in life."[11]

Boundary Building

So how do we manufacture these essential peripheries? Here are some tips.

1. *Identify the actions and behaviors that you find unacceptable.*[12] Tell people when they've acted in a way that insulted or degraded you. Be bold and tell people when you need time away from them or a situation. "Make a list of things that people may no longer do to you, say to you, or do around you. . . . Define your values, belief system, and outlook on life. . . . Get very clear on that."[13]

2. *Recognize that other people's needs and feelings are not more important than your own.*[14] You have the same right to feel positive, appreciated, and in control as everyone

---

10. Ibid.

11. "Boundaries in Relationships," http://lifeesteem.org/wellness/wellness_bound aries.html. Accessed July 22, 2015.

12. Hereford, "Healthy Boundaries."

13. Davenport, "10 Ways."

14. Hereford, "Healthy Boundaries."

else. Where you see that you have acquiesced in order to be accepted, begin asserting yourself—or, if necessary, cut yourself off from emotionally draining people who want to take, take, take.

3. *Learn to say no.*[15] When we try to please everyone—and RAs are pros at this—we find ourselves becoming unbalanced, unhealthy in body and spirit, and discouraged. You'll be amazed at what the word *no* will accomplish in your life!

4. *Realize that establishing boundaries is not selfish; it does not make you an uncaring person.*[16] Your self-esteem will grow as you decide how you want to be treated and offer yourself respect.

5. *Give yourself grace.* Skillfully building and maintaining boundaries takes time. When a person steps over or through your boundaries, speak up; make him or her aware, and tell the person to knock it off (respectfully, of course). "Walk away from any push-back or negative comments without acquiescing or getting angry. Over time, you and the other person will realize you're serious."[17]

6. *"Believe in yourself and your value as a unique individual who is worthy of love and respect. . . .* Practice self-confidence and self-love until it feels natural." Boundaries will help you do this.[18]

---

15. Ibid.

16. Davenport, "10 Ways."

17. Ibid.

18. Ibid.

7. *Determine that you will not be manipulated into doing things you don't want to do.* This is important especially when someone is trying to "guilt" you into submission.[19]
8. *Decide no one is allowed to shout at you, diminish your value, or call you names.*[20]
9. *Prioritize your own health and well-being.*[21]
10. *Keep your emotions separate from those of others.* But don't neglect empathy for those you love.[22]
11. *Acknowledge your own completeness.* Yes, the Bible says two are better than one, but that does not mean the one was incomplete before the other came along. It just means we were made for community, for connection, for mutual support. Our society's disastrously false notion that one person is just a "half" until someone comes along to "complete" him or her can lead to all kinds of unnecessary suffering.
12. *No longer let anyone determine your happiness and wholeness.* No wonder we chase, cling, and try to control other people. If those relationships end, so does our contentment—or so we fear. Be responsible for your own sense of well-being.

19. Adapted from "How to Establish Boundaries," http://www.wikihow.com/Establish-Boundaries. Accessed July 22, 2015.

20 Ibid.

21. Ibid.

22. Ibid.

A Template to Try

My friend Brian shared his experience with setting boundaries as he recovered from damaging relationships. Here are some guidelines he uses for navigating relationships:

- When someone shows you his character, believe him.
- Know that you can't control other people, but you can control what roles they play in your life.
- Realize you can't choose how people make you feel, but you can choose how you behave in response.[23]

We might find it helpful to apply this list to each important person in our lives. For example, ask yourself, *What behavior has my* (fill in the blank: spouse, pastor, sister, brother, coworker, boss) *shown that tells me who he/she is?* Remember, when you're setting boundaries you're looking at actions, not words. The actions should match the words and the image this person projects. After you write the list of behaviors, ask yourself: *Have I believed this person to be something different from what his or her actions tell me? To protect myself, do I need to erect a boundary between this person and myself?*

Maybe this person's behavior is exemplary and we desire to keep him or her close. Or maybe this person's behavior is troubling and so we recategorize the nature of our relationship. There are times when we need to change *inner circle friends* into *outer circle friends*—or even end or radically re-

---

23. Brian T. "Advice for the Abused." E-mail interview by author. March 17, 2015.

duce the time we spend on this friendship. For example, if a confidence we shared with a friend gets repeated to someone else, we know it's no longer safe to share personal information with that person. We then take whatever course of action we need to feel safe again. We may create space for ourselves by avoiding certain topics of conversation or even distancing ourselves emotionally, if necessary. Trust and safety are vital for healthy relationships, and if we no longer feel safe, we need to set some boundaries. The key to remember is that we can't control other people, or how they make us feel, but we can control what we do about them.

You're in Charge

It's important to remember that *we* decide what type of limits we set. Some boundaries are, figuratively speaking, thirty-foot-high rock walls with barbed wire on top (I've had only two people in my life who needed this kind of a boundary). Other boundaries are as nonrestrictive as picket fences. Sometimes I've set a picket-fence boundary only to discover that it needed to be a brick wall. Other times I've built a brick wall and later decided it could be a picket fence. No matter how we set our boundaries, we never have to apologize for putting some protection around ourselves.

Setting boundaries requires honesty. We may really want someone to stay in our lives, but if that person regularly makes us feel bad, we've got to be honest about it. Pretending others can't hurt us is like pretending we don't feel pain when someone steps on our toes. As Brian pointed out to me, the pain we feel is useful information from our emotions. We ignore that information at our own peril.[24]

I've had to place some pretty strong boundaries with abusive people—even members of my own family. Their behavior has shown me repeatedly that they don't care how badly they hurt me. Placing a powerful boundary with a parent, for example, is extra hard to do. We may feel as if we are dishonoring our parents. But sometimes, especially for children who grew up with religiously addicted parents, building a strong boundary is the only way we will recover our own spirituality.

Many addicts have had to end unhealthy relationships in order to make space for new, healthier ones. Relationship experts agree that the ability to *end* relationships is actually a sign of healthy interpersonal skills. Ended relationships are not failures. When moving forward without a particular relationship is better for our health and well-being, we can view ending it as a success.[25]

Just as the seasonal pruning of dead branches makes way for new growth, taking responsibility for our lives requires taking an inventory of our relationships and pruning back the ones that hinder our personal growth and spiritual sobriety.

No matter when or with whom we set boundaries, we often need to grieve the relationship that never was and never will be. Sometimes we don't miss the person so much as we miss the way we always hoped our relationship could be. Sometimes the loss is so painful and sobriety seems so

---

24. Brian T. "Advice for the Abused." E-mail interview by author. March 17, 2015.

25. Pia Mellody, *Facing Love Addiction: Giving Yourself the Power to Change the Way You Love* (New York: HarperOne, 2003), 159.

hopeless that we consider going back to our religiously addictive habits and relationships. I'm here to assure you that the pain *does* subside. It *does* get better. It's never too late to create—or resurrect—a health-giving boundary.

Good boundaries don't deprive us; they free us. The measure of freedom we experience is directly proportionate to the brawn of our boundaries. A boundary that is either too weak (causing us further injury) or too strong (preventing intimacy with another healthy person) will inhibit our freedom to pursue the lives we were meant to lead. With good boundaries, religious addicts begin to enjoy spiritual sobriety: they are freed to savor their lives and healthy, reciprocal, mutually fulfilling relationships in healthy ways.

Good boundaries are vital to our spiritual sobriety.

When to Forgive, and When to Reconcile

For most of my life, I couldn't tell where I started and others ended. I mentioned that when I was young, I suffered extreme physical and spiritual abuse. A significant aspect of my recovery as an addict was learning to forgive my abusers. Authors Henry Cloud and John Sims Townsend explain:

Many people have a problem determining the difference between forgiveness and reconciliation. . . . Do not think that because you have forgiven means you have to reconcile. You can offer reconciliation, but it must be contingent upon the other person owning her behavior and bringing forth trustworthy fruits. . . . Forgiveness is very hard. It means letting go of something that someone "owes" you. . . . Warning: *forgiveness and opening up to more abuse are not the same thing.* Forgiveness has to do with the past. Reconciliation and boundaries have to do with the future.[26]

Especially in spiritual environments people are told that reconciliation is the same thing as forgiveness. We are told we must accept the abuser's apology *and* allow him or her back into our lives. But it's actually harmful for us to reconcile with someone who hasn't demonstrated changed behavior, because it's a violation of our God-given rights and boundaries.

We *can* forgive. True forgiveness means releasing the person from his debt to us and doing so with an open heart, bearing no ill will or resentment. Honestly, it can be easier for us to remain in damaging, addictive situations than to forgive and move on without resentment, because at least in the relationship we know what to expect. But we also get to continue feeling sorry for ourselves because we're still victims. As my hairstylist, Gina, once told me, "Forgiveness has gotta be 100 percent, or that 1 percent will always run the show."

Letting go of the debt someone owes helps RAs to relax the clutches of guilt, shame, and resentment. I don't forgive someone because he or she deserves it. I forgive my abuser because *I* deserve it. I deserve to unload the backbreaking burden of unforgiveness. I deserve to release my heart and

26. Henry Cloud and John Townsend, *Boundaries: When to Say Yes, How to Say No to Take Control of Your Life* (Grand Rapids, MI: Zondervan Pub. House, 1992), 256, 257, 258, 268, 269.

mind and soul from the distress, obsessive thoughts, and fears that unforgiveness inflicts on me. I deserve to have my soul-space back to myself. Unforgiveness just takes up too much room! Yes, that person *hurt* me, but he or she didn't *destroy* me. Nobody has that kind of power. People have only as much power as we give them. And not forgiving our abusers is a big way we give them power.

In sobriety, we learn that forgiveness can be a form of self-care: we learn to let go of hurt because it helps us live healthier lives, not in order to help the offender or allow him or her back into our lives. As the popular Al-Anon daily reader, *Courage to Change*, suggests: We can't use forgiveness as a control mechanism whereby we "magnanimously bestow forgiveness" while still judging the other person. Instead, "the most forgiving thing I can do is remember that my job is not to judge others, but to think and behave in a way that lets me feel good."[27]

Forgiving others is also an opportunity for creating or reevaluating our boundaries. Are we placing ourselves in situations that might harm our physical, emotional, or spiritual safety? Do we need to place some physical distance between us and another person, place, or thing? Perhaps we need to write down exactly what happened, so if a similar situation arises we'll remember what happened the first time. By exercising meaningful personal boundaries, we learn that a big part of trusting others means trusting them *appropriately* and in a way that lets us live safely.

27. Al-Anon Family Groups, *Courage to Change* (Virginia Beach, VA: Al-Anon Family Group Headquarters, 1992), 75.

But even if we completely forgive those who hurt us, we are not obligated to reconcile with them. In fact, we may never see or talk to them again. Though I forgave him, I waited years for my cult-founding grandfather to repent—to call and apologize. I waited . . . and waited. Then one day he just died. And that was that: No reconciliation. No changed behavior. I cried for a little bit, and then suddenly I wasn't crying anymore. His life had ended the way he'd lived it. Twelve years previous, he'd shown me who he was and I had believed it. I had moved on with my life.

In many ways, I actually felt sorry for him. How tragic to be so lost in religious addiction that you can never get spiritually sober. How isolating it must feel that even when hundreds of people are telling you the truth, you earnestly and sincerely believe all of them are wrong. How terrifying to hate yourself so much that you'd rather lose everything you worked your whole life to build than admit you have a problem. If that isn't hell, I don't know what is.

This is how we forgive our abusers: we allow ourselves to see their humanity. I forgave my abusers because I realized that they weren't evil; they were simply terribly sick people. Indeed, my grandfather's case of religious addiction was so severe that it was fatal.

Perhaps my hope that he'd get sober was really the hope that I'd get sober. After all, I was never in charge of his recovery. The only recovery I could ever own was my own. The only person I could ever save was myself. I couldn't repent for him. But I could repent myself. I couldn't undo the damage he'd done, but I could make sure I didn't repeat his behavior.

Each of us must make our own journey of spiritual sobriety, regardless of whether we go alone or others join us. We don't need to wait for harmful people to change or apologize before we make this journey. But we also won't make much progress *unless* we forgive them—even if that means we never see them again. And that's okay. Parting ways may even be the best option for us.

We hold the keys to our own happiness and creating spiritually sober relationships.

Practice Your Spiritual Sobriety

Prayer:

God grant me the courage to acknowledge the pain I've suffered in religiously addictive relationships. Grant me the courage to forgive those who harmed me, the compassion to forgive myself, and the strength and wisdom I need to live in freedom and safety. Amen.

Promise:

"But with you there is forgiveness, so that we can, with reverence, serve you." Psalm 130:4, NIV

Journaling/Group Questions:
- Sometimes ending a relationship is the very definition of success. Are there relationships in your life that no longer—or never did—edify your spiritual well-being? Can you identify relationships in your life that may need pruning?
- What is the difference between forgiveness and reconciliation?
- How is forgiveness important to building boundaries?

- Is it hard for you to believe God's love for you is unconditional? What is hindering you from accepting this kind of love?
- List three boundaries you can erect to show unconditional love toward yourself.
- List three ways you can show unconditional love for others.

8

True Religion

Recovery in Our Churches

I see the church as a field hospital after battle. It is useless to ask a seriously injured person if he has high cholesterol or about the level of his blood sugars. You have to heal his wounds. Then we can talk about everything else.

—POPE FRANCIS

THIRTY YEARS AGO, THE CHURCH NOW KNOWN AS HILLSONG was a small Pentecostal Assemblies of God in the suburbs of Sydney, Australia. Today, Hillsong boasts churches in fifteen countries, and its worship band—Hillsong United—dominates Christian music charts. If you've attended a contemporary church service in the last five years, you've probably sung a Hillsong worship composition. As the *New York Times* observed, Hillsong churches have become a magnet for young Christians, "combining the production values of a rock concert, the energy of a nightclub and the community of a megachurch."[1]

Hillsong isn't the only Protestant church to experience explosive growth in the last few decades. In America, there has been a 400 percent increase in Protestants who iden-

1. Michael Paulson, "Megachurch with a Beat Lures a Young Flock," *New York Times*, September 9, 2014. Accessed May 4, 2015. http://www.nytimes.com/2014/09/10/us/hillsong-megachurch-with-a-beat-lures-a-young-flock.html.

tify as nondenominational.[2] Indeed, the fastest growing churches are unaffiliated with any traditional Christian denomination.[3] In some ways, it seems the nondenominational church has become its own denomination. And yet, all this growth is at odds with recent religious surveys.

A 2015 survey by the Pew Research Center found that, overall, the number of Americans who described themselves as Christian had dropped nearly 8 percentage points since 2007.[4] What is happening? Is Christianity really declining in the United States, or is church growth simply happening in unaccounted-for sectors of the population?

A little bit of both. According to Pew, the decline in Christians "has been driven mainly by declines among mainline Protestants and Catholics."[5] But what may not be obvious is that while an increasing number of people identify as "none"—meaning they have no religious affiliation—many of them still have a thriving personal spiritual practice.

For my part, I'm Catholic but not dogmatic. My religious practice is guided by ancient Christian tradition while my spirituality ensures I remain openhearted and not legalistic. I find great solace in treading the old paths worn smooth by

2. Ed Stetzer, "The Rise of the Evangelical 'nones'—CNN.com," CNN, June 12, 2015. Accessed June 26, 2015. http://www.cnn.com/2015/06/12/living/stetzer -christian-nones/index.html.

3. Russell D. Moore, "Where Have All the Presbyterians Gone?" *WSJ*, February 4, 2011. Accessed June 26, 2015. http://www.wsj.com/articles/SB1000142405274870 3437304576120690548462776.

4. Brian Naylor, "Christians in U.S. on Decline As Number of 'Nones' Grows, Survey Finds," NPR, May 12, 2015. Accessed June 27, 2015. http://www.npr .org/sections/thetwo-way/2015/05/12/406154155/christians-in-u-s-on-decline-as -number-of-nones-grows-survey-finds.

5. Ibid.

saints gone before me. But I also find immeasurable grace in developing my own relationship with God.

Ultimately, the spiritual health of a church isn't determined by whether it has "the energy of a night club" or experiences rapid growth. It takes a lifetime to become a sincere, mature follower of Christ—a healthy church structure reflects that.

It seems possible that megachurches create more religious addicts than faithful Christians, because when high-intensity experiences are emphasized over solid catechesis and traditional Christian sacraments, true religion is lost.

True religion isn't glamorous, exciting, sexy, or showy. True religion, as the Bible defines it, means feeding the poor, taking care of widows, and keeping ourselves detached from the world. Those things are patently *unglamorous*. Most of the time, in fact, gospel work is quite simply invisible work.

In chapter 1 we looked at the danger religious highs pose to the individual. But now I'd like us to consider more closely how an experience-driven religious practice affects the health of a church body. In other words, when a church focuses on style, relevance, and mass appeal to an entertainment-saturated culture, what is it sacrificing? When a church is run more like a production company and less like a house of worship, can we rightly even call it a "church"?

Spiritually Sober Church Defined

In her book, *Searching for Sunday*, Rachel Held Evans writes that young people aren't actually looking for a *hipper* Christianity, but a *truer* one. "Like every generation before ours and every generation after, we're looking for Jesus, . . . who can be found in the strange places he's always been found: in bread, in wine, in baptism, in the Word, in suffering, in community, and among the least of these. No coffee shops or fog machines required."[6]

A truer Christian practice is focused not on events, concerts, or experiences but on devotion to teaching, fellowship, prayer, serving others, and the sacraments of our faith: baptism, confirmation, Eucharist, confession, anointing of the sick, holy orders, and marriage. In other words, a sober spirituality is not focused on me and my personal experience but on *us together*, practicing the sacred mysteries of the church universal.

Pastor Michael Helms notes that church attendance—something addicts can turn into a compulsion—may get in the way of real ministry to others:

> It seems that some Christians attend church meetings disproportionately to the amount of time that's actually spent serving others—you know, being the church. . . . Many have become keepers of the aquarium instead of fishers of men. Dropping money in the offering plate to send people to Africa or to the Middle East is different from interacting with and ministering to someone of another race or culture in your own community.[7]

6. Rachel Held Evans, *Searching for Sunday: Loving, Leaving, and Finding the Church* (Nashville: Thomas Nelson, 2015), xii.

7. Michael Helms, "Some Folks Need to Break Their Addiction—to Church," March 26, 2009, http://www.ethicsdaily.com/some-folks-need-to-break-their-addiction-to-church-cms-13950#sthash.Ct5oS0gA.dpuf. Accessed July 27, 2015.

Helms suggests a healthier approach, a return to biblically illustrated true religion: "What if churches had this rule: 'For every hour you spend at the church house, you must spend one hour in the community ministering to the poor, taking care of the needy, attending to the least of these?'"[8] That would be a spiritually sober (and supernaturally effective) church. It's just what we addicts need.

You see, a spiritually sober church never cuts its spotlight on the essentials of faith. Mass religious movements that explode in popularity over a short period of time often neglect several of these essentials. Even the most lavish worship band concert is no substitute for the richness of a life renewed through baptism. No conference, no bestselling book, no sold-out arena can compare to the body of Christ, broken for us. This is because true religion, and true spiritual sobriety, can never be bought or sold. Spiritual sobriety is the slow, difficult work of walking the narrow way.

Of course, the addict in us may want to make a grand, splashy gesture and commit everything to Jesus. But here's the thing: Jesus doesn't want our big, showy, public surrenders. In fact, emotionally fraught, stadium-style altar calls and gospel meetings can do more harm than good because they make a grand, public performance of what should be a private, inner transformation.

We can hold conferences and stage concerts. We can dress in hip clothing and dim the lights and turn up the music. But I believe recovery in our churches means deemphasizing these things, because we don't control spiritual transforma-

8. Ibid.

tion. God does. We can plan and strategize and form com-
mittees to figure out ways to save the lost and change the
world—or we can just do it, one person at a time.

Recovery in our churches happens when we welcome
the socially awkward, totally-not-hip, insecure, marginalized,
broken people of this world—including ourselves—and simply offer what Christianity has always offered: the healing
body and blood of Jesus.

Where Grace Is Found

In her early teens, Samantha became a congregational pianist
for her church. She'd been taking piano lessons since age
five, and by the time she began playing in church, she was a
talented pianist.

"Being able to do that—to glorify God with my talent in
order to help my church worship Him—was something I
cherished," Samantha recalled. "But then I developed ten-
donitis in both wrists. Playing at that volume for a sustained
period of time was too much strain while my body tried to
heal. Finally, under the advice of my doctor and physical
therapist, I stopped playing for the church."

When the pastor's wife heard that Samantha was still taking piano lessons, she told Samantha she was sinning. "She
berated me for letting my 'pride' get in the way of serving
God," Samantha shared. "She said God would destroy my talent if I didn't use it primarily in church. I tried to explain that
I didn't *want* to stop playing for church, but I was obeying my
parents and trying to preserve my ability to play the piano at
all. She didn't listen. Before she walked away she said to me:

'God is not mocked.' A few months later, the pastor preached a sermon about the proper use of our talents and used me as an example of someone who had forsaken the worship of God. That utterly broke me."[9]

I have heard so many stories similar to Samantha's where, instead of demonstrating grace, church leadership dished out judgment and condemnation. It shouldn't be this way. Pastors are shepherds, not emperors. They simply shouldn't have so much power that they are free to shame, threaten, and manipulate their flock. The greatest danger to a church's spiritual health is a pastor-centric church model.

If you've roamed in evangelical circles, you've probably heard the advice that finding a "good" church means finding a Bible-teaching church. But is this the only criteria necessary for a healthy church? Churches that revolve around the preaching gifts of one person set themselves up for failure. What happens when that pastor retires? Or resigns from ministry? Or worse, falls prey to moral failure? Solid biblical instruction is just one facet of a healthy church.

If you want to know whether a church is healthy, look at the how it treats people who have little or nothing to offer. Are the homeless welcomed? Are the disabled offered a front-row seat? Do children look forward to going to church? Does the socially awkward college student get invited to coffee? Would members of the LGBT community feel safe attending services?

If you're looking for a spiritually sober church, look for grace.

9. "Faith Used as a Weapon." Online interview by author. April 14, 2015.

Portraits of Healthy Churches

I asked some of my blog readers to share their experiences in healthy churches. See if you can spot the common characteristics:

> We are in a church now that we love! They have paid elders and lay elders, they have the congregation vote and weigh in on everything, they are totally transparent on finances (including salaries), and the church votes on changes to the budget, too; [and] there are women serving in pretty much every area of the church (except preaching). It is the least judgmental or legalistic church I've ever been part of. —Didi

> The church I am in right now is the first that resonates as home. Quite simply [it is] about the things that matter: people and the gospel. We have men who serve in kids' ministries and women who preach and are elders. They care for the community they are in, including the homeless men around the church in the mornings. They invite them to be active participants in the service. They care for the "least of these," the marginalized and those who are really [messed up]. The pastors are well read, thoughtful, caring, and genuine. Above all they are eclectic. There is no one right type among them; they represent the diversity that is the body of Christ. Finances are super-transparent and are always dealt with in a spirit of generosity and coming alongside God's work of redemp-

tion, never with guilt or pressure or using the dreaded word "tithe." —Jessica

I'm LGBTQ, and needless to say, I've had a few bad experiences with church. The church I go to now is so open and loving. I cried the first few times I went there. I was so used to fighting pastors at the other churches, and I came here and I didn't want to fight anymore. I feel so safe and loved.—Amanda

Before I moved I went to a healthy church and I would describe it as:

- financially transparent.
- [having] no need to be fake.
- [a place where] all ages were cared for spiritually.
- [a place without] a culture of fear/condemnation.
- not afraid of change.
- accountable.
- [having a] commitment to following the Bible, not tradition.
- accepting. Not of sin, but people in general. —Jackie

The church that had the most impact on my life so far made me feel incredibly safe and wanted. The biggest [difference] is that they didn't shame or silence people who had doubt or questions. [They let people ask] not just the safe questions that can be answered by a Bible verse, but the big, scary questions: Is God real? Is Jesus really who we think He is? When I moved elsewhere and searched for another church, I looked for the doubters. If they're welcomed, then I will be too. —Gina[10]

From these stories and many others I've found that the three clearest identifiers of a healthy church are

1. A loving acceptance of all people.
2. Financial transparency.
3. Leadership accountability.

When just one of these characteristics is missing, things go badly and people get hurt. Of course, healthy churches have many other positive attributes, but these three things are vital.

Here's an important tip: it shouldn't be difficult to ascertain whether a church meets these criterion. Healthy churches are open, honest, and accessible. It should be obvious on your first visit whether a church is loving and accepting: you will feel welcomed. Plurality and diversity of leadership should be easy to identify: you will recognize the people who are in charge and they won't all look, talk, or act the same. You shouldn't need some kind of security clearance to access information about church finances. Only unhealthy churches are opaque about money matters. And if things seem okay on the surface but your gut tells you something is off, don't disregard that uneasiness.

10. "What Does a Healthy Church Look Like?" Online interview by author. May 4, 2015.

Many horror stories begin, "I felt like something was weird in that church but I ignored it because everyone seemed so happy." As Brian said in the last chapter, truly, we ignore such feelings to our own detriment. And if we override our qualms enough times, the danger is that we will become accustomed to an unhealthy environment. We will begin to think judgmental behavior is normal—even good. We will begin believing we don't need to know what the leadership is doing with the money.

Never underestimate the power of group dynamics. Once you're inside the church and functioning as a full-fledged member, it's much harder to see what's truly going on. As an outsider, you have the most objective perspective.

What Should You Do?

Maybe you're asking, *Should I stay in the church I attend and try to change things from the inside, or should I leave and find a healthier church?* What is the savvy choice for an addict pursuing sobriety? Only you can answer that. Some have to leave the churches where they became addicted; some can stay and change their use of and participation in that church. People vary. And our sober needs vary. As with any other aspect of recovery, do what is best for you.

Some of my closest RA friends have walked away from church. They realized that they could not remain in a church context and get the recovery they needed. These friends remain some of the kindest, most spiritually attuned people I know. Others are able to stay in their respective churches and work for institutional change. A friend of mine, Carrie, once told me that even though her feminist ideas sometimes get her into trouble with other Mormons, she stays in her church because "If I'm not here, who will say the things that need to be said?"[11]

Regardless of whether we stay, leave, or just take a break from church, we can always work our recovery because spiritual sobriety isn't dependent on church attendance; it's only dependent on our willingness to work with a loving God.

Practice Your Spiritual Sobriety

Prayer:
God, grant us an understanding of your love that we may carry it to our churches or identify it at other churches. Help us know where we do and don't belong. Show us how to define sober religious practice.

Promise:
"The man who loves God is known by God." I Corinthians 8:3, NIV

Journaling/Group Questions:
- Name some of the problems you've seen in experience-driven, high-intensity churches.
- Name a few positive things that have come from these churches.
- What do you think constitutes a healthy, spiritually sober church?
- Do you agree or disagree that fewer programs and more practicing

11. "Staying in Church." Telephone interview by author. May 30, 2015.

of the sacraments is conducive to nurturing a thriving spirituality? Why or why not?

- Why is it important for churches to rely less on conferences, concerts, and events?
- What does every religious addict truly need? Why? As you pursue sobriety, how will you seek this?

9

Speed Bump

Relapse

Between stimulus and response there is a space.
In that space is our power to choose our response.
In our response lies our growth and our freedom.

—*VIKTOR FRANKL*

My Recovery To-Do List

1. Use your day planner. People (especially your kids) are sick of hearing "I forgot."
2. Quit saying the f-word.
3. Get over disgust with Pinterest. Make *good* crafts with kids at least 1x/wk.
4. Sew new school dresses for twins, but finish all the other ones first.
5. Use your dessert cookbook—no more lazy cookies from the recipe on the back of the Nestlé bag (and, yes, *of course* this means no more canned cookie dough).
6. LOSE. WEIGHT. *Never* take this one off the list, obviously.
7. Exercise every day.
8. Quit texting you-know-who. If she doesn't text back, don't take it personally. Just STOP texting her forgodssakes.
9. Stop complaining about that new Common Core curriculum

and just learn it already so that you can help with the kids' math homework.

10. WRITE A GRATITUDE LIST LIKE ALL THE OTHER HAPPY PEOPLE.

11. Earn more money.

12. Learn a foreign language.

13. Take the dog to vet for that weird head-shaking thing.

14. *Us Weekly* doesn't count as nonfiction reading material. Read a REAL book.

15. Less selfies on Instagram.

16. More Bible w/coffee pix.

17. Set iPhone alerts for 3x daily prayer.

18. Volunteer at kid's school more.

19. JUST DO MORE OF EVERYTHING.

20. Except the bad stuff. Do *less* of that.

Oh, hello there. This is me. Relapsing. Trying so earnestly to work my recovery that I'm crashing and burning all over the place.

No, really.

Listen, recovery isn't automatic good behavior and healthy choices. It's up and down; three steps forward, two steps back—you know the clichés. You're going to fail—a lot. And you're going to get back up. And then you're going to fail again. And really, it's very okay.

In recovery, there are bloopers.

A lot of them.

Here's a counterintuitive principle of recovery: working hard at being good leads to relapse. Yep. I learned that the hard way.

If there's anything to be gleaned from the recurring public scandals of religious people, it's that trying to be holy only creates bigger hypocrites. Sadly, trying to be holy is often what we religious addicts do best!

Most religious addicts I've known are high achievers. Among other addicts, we are the nerds of the group. We usually have a very strong work ethic (in fact, we're probably as addicted to work as we are to religion). We truly believe there's no problem that can't be fixed with a little elbow grease and perseverance. "Being good" is encoded in our religious DNA. Nobody loves order, cleanliness, and efficiency more than we do. We adore our lists, our spreadsheets, and our strategies for managing the unmanageable.

The problem is that religious addiction, like any addiction, doesn't respond well to spreadsheets. We may trick ourselves into believing we're facing our addictive behaviors simply because we stay so busy making rules, creating personal mission statements, and tracking our behavior on daily charts. But recovering junkies often mistake productivity for progress. Our addiction isn't cured or resolved just because we repress our behaviors into neat little to-do lists—or do nothing at all.

What we need in recovery is a different strategy altogether. I'm going to suggest that we do something really radical, uncomfortable, and borderline blasphemous: *we stop trying to be good.*

Exchange Good for Honest

As most addicts will tell you, getting sober isn't hard but *staying* sober is. For religious addicts, the best way to prevent relapse is to stop working so hard at being good—i.e., attempting to attain unrealistic versions of holiness. What would happen if we replaced striving to be completely obedient with a more relaxed approach to life? What would happen if we stopped trying to be better behaved and instead focused on being more honest?

This reminds me of Jesus's words in the gospel of St. Matthew: "First wash the inside of the cup and the dish, and then the outside will become clean, too."[1] If we can find a way to be honest, then we are washing the inside of the cup. Perhaps all God asks of us is humble honesty because *He's* the one who makes us good.

There's such relief in honesty. For one thing, it's a lot less stressful. Being honest unburdens us from needing to keep track of our lies or hide our secrets. When we're honest, we don't obsess about our mistakes or feel compelled to punish ourselves with forty-day fasts or new promises to try harder. When we're honest, we no longer obsess about how we're the chief of all sinners! Only pride tells us we're the worst. Honesty helps us discover we're just human, kinda like everyone else.

Honesty is the fastest path to goodness, because it is the most direct path to God. Every religious addict I've ever known is truly starving for God. We so desperately want to find Him. But maybe if we just get honest, God will actually find us.

Why is it so hard for religious addicts to be honest? First, as RAs we often set ourselves up as the voices of religious authority and therefore have a vested interest in appear-

1. Matthew 23:26, NLT.

ing spotless and "above reproach." We fear we are held to a higher moral standard than ordinary mortals. If we fail, we may disappoint and hurt others because they look up to us. Our failures could even cause others to lose their faith.

Second, being honest is difficult for us because we may have been punished for it in the past. Maybe we learned that others prefer their *idea* of us rather than the reality. Maybe we've lost friends or jobs or people's trust because we've spoken honestly. Maybe we've seen others chastened for their honesty—for admitting their failures or suggesting others have flaws. Whatever the case, we may believe that honesty is not the best policy.

And so we hide.

And the more we hide, the more we repress.

And the more we repress, the more we obsess.

Until one day we relapse.

Relapse, and the Instant Cure/Conversion

For me, relapse means my return to the RA's emotional volatility and obsession. From the outside, it looks like struggle: me trying compulsively to fix people and things, running around all frantic and busy, busy, busy. I stop praying. I don't ask God for help. I feel like I have to do this all on my own.

For other religious addicts, relapse means a return to behaviors that addiction experts describe as *ritualizing*. For RAs this might include rigid adherence to religious rules, finding fault with others' beliefs, trying urgently to "prove" points of doctrine, attending an excessive number of religious services, or plunging into volunteer church work.

Essentially, relapse for any addict means a return to seeking relief in externals: people, places, or things. Being *intoxicated* means we are engaging in behaviors that we've previously identified as compromising our sobriety and, ultimately, our sanity.

Relapse is also accompanied by a remarkable lapse in self-care. I stop brushing my teeth—not to mention flossing. Some don't brush their hair for days. Others eat poorly and sleep less. Some don't exercise. (See chapter 6 for more on self-care.) For me, the biggest indicator of relapse is going several days without journaling, which has always been a way for me to check in with myself, to express what I'm going through, and to get honest. When I don't journal, it's a sure sign that I'm losing myself. During my biggest relapse, I didn't journal for several years.

When I think about what leads to my relapse in spiritual sobriety, I can identify one faulty belief that set me up for failure: the instant cure/conversion.

Growing up as an evangelical-fundamentalist-born-again believer, I was taught that God transformed people's lives *immediately*. Our salvation would come to us like St. Paul's on the road to Damascus: God's dazzling brilliance strikes us and BOOM! we're converted!

When I was a young teenager growing up in Orange County, California, I attended a harvest crusade being held in a local baseball stadium. Oh, what a religious high that was! There were thousands of cheering Christians, soaring music, and a witty, charismatic preacher working that crowd like a professional performer. He told stories that made us laugh and made us weep. We heard personal testimonies about God delivering people from drug and alcohol addiction as soon as they'd received Jesus. The preacher promised that life was better and happier with Jesus, that all it took to have this amazing new life was one simple prayer.

The whole message of the evening was that no matter what we'd done, our lives could be immediately transformed right here, right now. When the preacher invited people to come and ask Jesus into their hearts, I watched as thousands of people streamed down onto the baseball field.

I never went onto the field myself, because I'd already asked Jesus into my heart about eight thousand times. But each summer, I attended the harvest crusade because I discovered I could get a contact high just by watching other people get drunk on God. Even though the from-darkness-into-marvelous-light moment had never happened for me, I still wanted to believe it was possible. I still wanted to believe the seductive promise that God grants right-here, right-now transformations.

But this kind of theology often backfires for those of us who were raised in church. "I used to wish I'd been born into a non-Christian family so I would have more sin to repent of than just not being kind to my brother," Sandra wrote on my Facebook page. "I was so envious of the drunks and druggies and people who'd lived promiscuously (for one thing, their lives sounded far more fun than I'd ever known) because they had such clear conversions. I couldn't even give a date for my 'spiritual birthday.'"[2]

2. "What Was Your Conversion Experience Like?" Online interview by author. April 21, 2015.

Others spoke of how their salvation didn't seem to matter as much because it didn't cause a big shift in their lives. "I still feel like I must have done it wrong somehow because the transformation in my life has been so slow, and I can't always tell there's change," Brenda wrote in an e-mail. "I feel like a fraud because it's still so hard. It's like I was already a part of the flock so it wasn't a big deal that I wanted to be in it. I felt like God wanted really bad people to become Christians so other people could see His power. But I wasn't useful because I was the good kid who had been in church my whole life."[3]

The dramatic conversion is an idea that would haunt me, too, as I tried to maintain my spiritual sobriety. I guess I'd been hoping that rehab would be my transformation experience, that I'd be "cured." Despite the therapists telling me that wasn't how recovery worked, I still clung to the impossible hope that the instant cure *could* happen to me because I was different from other addicts—I believed in Jesus.

I thought about getting cured the same way a gambler thinks about winning the lottery. The odds are millions to one, but it doesn't matter. We still *believe*.

From Instant Cures to Real Ones

The reality was that while rehab saved me from destroying my life, it didn't save me from *living* it—which is to say, someone still had to wash the dishes and get the kids to school on time. The hard truth of spiritual sobriety is that God doesn't

3. "Conversion Experience." E-mail message to author. April 21, 2015.

rescue us from our problems or circumstances. Spiritual so-briety, perhaps like conversion, isn't about the big moments but rather the slow journey of daily choices made one day at a time.

The good news is that you're not alone. You're not the only believer who has ever doubled back to church for another contact high. You're not the only one who, despite years of church and obedience, feels spiritually lost in a barren wil-derness. You're not the only one who has tried to earn God's approval via unhesitating obedience and 100 percent sub-mission, only to feel let down and disillusioned. All of us have felt these things at one time or another. And all of us have slipped and fallen—then fallen again. What I want you to know is that relapsing is okay. It's just a part of our conver-sion journey.

And when we relapse, we might not always make an instantaneous return to our sobriety. Religious addiction doesn't respond very well to sudden movements, so to speak. Coming down hard on ourselves and setting up a stringent "recovery checklist" (like the one I wrote at the beginning of this chapter) will probably backfire. Instead, just as with the gradual process of conversion, we are allowed to take our time. Once we've identified the addictive behaviors we've re-engaged, we may need to slowly wean ourselves off them.

For many of us, this gradual sobriety process may feel confusing, especially in our culture of fast-paced change and achievement. But take heart, the idea of immediate cures and conversion is actually a fairly recent development in church history, started by evangelical preachers like D. L. Moody in the late 1800s, popularized by born-again Christians during the Jesus Movement, and made ubiquitous by televangelists from the 1980s until today.

When I asked my readers to describe their conversion experiences, a man named Ross shared that he was uncomfortable with what he called "the Hollywood, red-carpet testimonies [that] never seemed to match the person I knew behind the scenes." For him, the instant Christian narrative seemed false. "It was performance art at its best, I guess. My conversion was just *me*—exposed and vulnerable."[4]

Maybe being "just me" is all we need. We don't have to impress anybody or put on a show. We don't have to show up at some public event to declare our faith—in fact, those kinds of intense, emotional activities feed our religious addiction. There's nowhere we have to be on this journey except right here, right now. We have permission to take a break, take a walk. We have permission to throw away our checklists and spreadsheets. Could it be that the idea of instant transformation says more about our society's obsession with instant gratification than it does about the quality of our pursuit of sobriety?

Sobriety is about gentle self-examination and, most of all, a desire to stop living in pain. We choose it because addiction is a painful and depressing way of life. We choose it because we are sick to death of our compulsive behaviors.

And, even if the conversion isn't an instant one, in choosing spiritual sobriety we choose freedom.

---

4. "What Was Your Conversion Experience Like?" Online interview by author. April 21, 2015.

Don't Trade One Addiction for Another

Addictions refuse to be *managed*. They can, however, be covered up—usually with another addiction. As RA expert Richard Minor observes, "The Christian Church's ongoing obsession with sex and sexuality, the centrality it has put on controlling and forbidding sexuality in its message of sinfulness, is a suspicious sign that religious addiction and sexual addiction have been regularly reinforcing each other."[5]

Is it any coincidence that most of the scandals involving religious people involve sexual behavior? I don't think so. Sex addiction experts agree that repression often leads to obsession, and obsession often leads to acting out. In other words, imposing strict rules on ourselves and doubling down on corralling our "bad" behavior is only going to make things worse.

We touched on this in chapter 6, but I want to take another look at this issue in light of relapse.

Responding to a survey I conducted about religious addiction, Sandra wrote:

> I went from being sure that "declaring Jesus as Lord" would save the world to being sure that eating organic and locally grown food, birthing, raising, and educating my children "holistically" and teaching others to do the same was the salvation of our future. I was far more evangelistic in my new crusade than I ever had been for Jesus—I preached the sermons of clean eating and clean

5. Robert N. Minor, *When Religion Is an Addiction* (St. Louis, MO: Humanity Works!, 2007), 78.

living to everyone I met. . . . Instead of accruing heav-
enly "crowns of righteousness" and the approbation of
the religious community, I scored righteous hippy points
by being the most holy mother in the co-op.[6]

Sandra's story reflects a common theme among people
leaving religiously addictive environments: we tend to leave
one extreme environment and jump right into another. We
have become so accustomed to extremism that healthy relationships seem boring. To us, healthy people with good
boundaries are not attractive because they don't need us to
rescue them.

My friend Brian says that growing up in a spiritually
extreme church gave him an "absurdly high tolerance for
abuse."[7] It's disconcerting for us to realize that if we are
to have emotionally and spiritually sound relationships, we
must give up the junk food of drama and develop a healthier
palate. My therapist once told me I would know I was pro-
gressing in my recovery when my tolerance for abusive behavior diminished.

Some religious addicts give up fundamentalism and take
up extreme exercise regimens. Others became crusaders for
veganism, sustainable living, or holistic medicines. In an article for the *Washington Post,* author Ragan Sutterfield identified the similarities between zealous CrossFit athletes and
religious cults:

6. "Survey Questionnaire for Spiritual Sobriety." E-mail interview by author.
April 25, 2015.

7. "Advice for the Abused." E-mail interview by author. March 17, 2015.

CrossFit, for all its popularity or perhaps because of it, has had a slew of detractors. Many critics scrutinize its rigorous methods. Others worry about the semi-religious fervor devotees seem to bring to the sport. "CrossFit is a cult," someone might say. Or, "CrossFit is a religion." The accusations are understandable for those who have had a friend or relative become a regular member of a box (CrossFit parlance for a gym). There's a kind of dedication, a gleam in the eye that many don't find in a weekly Zumba class.[8]

Don't get me wrong. I think exercise is crucial to our physical, emotional, and mental well-being. A few years ago, I even joined a fitness boot camp. I absolutely loved it— especially the runner's high. In a blog post from 2013, I realized the dangerous exchange I'd made:

> One year ago, in addition to a physical breakdown, I was suffering a spiritual crisis. I was disillusioned. My usual method for restarting my spirituality was praying more, fasting more, reading Scripture more. Except this time, I couldn't do that. It wasn't working. I stopped praying. I stopped fasting. I stopped reading Scripture. Instead, I went running.[9]

8. Ragan Sutterfield, "The Cult of CrossFit: How the Workout Can Bring out the Best (and Worst) of Faith," *Washington Post,* March 24, 2015. http://www.washingtonpost.com/news/acts-of-faith/wp/2015/03/24/the-cult-of-crossfit-how-the-workout-can-bring-out-the-best-and-worst-of-faith/.

9. Elizabeth Esther. "How Running Saved My Life & Faith." Elizabeth Esther (blog), January 31, 2013. www.elizabethesther.com.

Running changed my life. It helped me realize that I could meet difficult challenges. I lost weight and felt amazing. But like most addicts, I took it too far. After going all out in boot camp for a year and a half, I began experiencing constant pain in my left knee. Every time I ran, it felt "crunchy." A few months later, a physical therapist informed me I was very close to seriously injuring my left knee. I had to quit boot camp for several months and give my body a chance to heal.

Running was great exercise, but by treating it as a "religion" of sorts, I used it to replace the spiritual high I got from religious addiction. I still needed God—especially after I couldn't run for a while—and I still needed to learn how to live without extremes.

Helpful Tips After a Slip

If you've experienced a momentary lapse in your sobriety or a full-blown relapse, getting back on track can feel overwhelming. We may feel ashamed that we've slipped up *again*. We may feel there's no hope for us. We may believe we've permanently damaged our relationship with God, others, and ourselves. These thoughts and feelings may actually prevent us from recommitting to sobriety.

We need to know that no matter how often we fall, there is *always* hope for renewed sobriety.

Here are some ideas:

- Talk to a trusted friend, spiritual director, or support group about what happened.
- Write down the ways your addiction re-manifested itself.

- Describe the unmanageability it caused in your life.
- Listen to the stories of others as a way to regain hope for change.
- Ask God for help.
- Accept the help and suggestions of those who are familiar with your story.
- Call others who have struggled similarly—even just calling to say hi and leaving a short, encouraging message helps two people: It helps you get out of your obsessive thinking. And your encouraging words give someone else hope for change.
- Forgive yourself.
- Practice self-care: take a bath, read a book, take the dog for a walk.
- Ask yourself if you're doing too much for others.
- Avoid triggering situations, persons, and things (high-intensity spiritual experiences, close contact with other religious addicts, books, or websites that trigger intense religious feeling).
- Ask for God's forgiveness.
- Remember: you are not alone!

When we've relapsed, it's vital that we refrain from self-loathing, because self-loathing leads to even more self-destructive behaviors. Relapse is disappointing, but it doesn't have to be devastating. After all, even the most sober person is sober only one day at a time. Today is always the day of salvation. It's never too late to start over.

And so we begin, and begin again.

Reignite Your Spiritual Sobriety

Prayer:

God, when we've fallen, help us stand. When we've failed, give us strength to try again. Establish our sobriety and help us protect it.

Promise:

"Even though good people may be bothered by trouble seven times, they are never defeated." Proverbs 24:16 NCV

Journaling/Group Questions:

How can you avoid relapse? What issues tempt you the most? What warning signs can you be aware of?

- Make a plan for times you may slip in your sobriety. Whom can you call for support? What will you do about the source of temptation? What resources can help you get back on track? To whom will you be accountable as you restart your sober journey?

- In times of relapse, manage your self-talk: no berating, no name-calling, no Shame-Braining. What can you say to yourself that puts relapse into perspective and sparks you back into sobriety?

10

Good Enough

A Last Word

HISTORY IS FULL OF MEN AND WOMEN WHO HAVE LIVED spiritually sober lives. Because they were humble, moderate, gentle, and disciplined, it's easy to assume these calm, sober people were endowed with special powers. But that would be a mistake. Spiritual sobriety isn't just for mystics and contemplatives. It's for all of us. In fact, I'd say the most precious examples of spiritual sobriety are often overlooked precisely because they are so plain and ordinary.

The Bible tells us we have this treasure in "jars of clay."[1] There's nothing fancy or special about clay jars. They aren't shiny. They don't attract attention. They're breakable. And yet, as the great English poet William Wordsworth might say, the "outward semblance doth belie Thy soul's immensity."[2] In

---

1. 2 Corinthians 4:7, NIV.

2. William Wordsworth. "536. Ode. Intimations of Immortality. William Wordsworth. The Oxford Book of English Verse." Bartleby.com Great Books Online. Accessed July 3, 2015. http://www.bartleby.com/101/536.html.

other words, don't let appearances fool you; the small, mortal human body contains the immense, eternal soul.

Spiritually sober people often aren't necessarily famous or glamorous. But all of them have grappled with the painful problem of addiction and discovered that filling the emptiness with anything other than God's love leads only to suffering. True love—real, deep, soul-quenching love—fills us up completely. And when we are full, we don't crave junk food. This is what the love of God can do for us, if we let it: it can fill up the soul's immensity from top to bottom.

In his letter to the Ephesians, St. Paul writes that we are "filled up to all the fullness of God" when we come to know the love of Christ.[3] This is the fullness our souls long for, the fullness St. John speaks of in his Gospel: "For of His fullness have we all received, and grace upon grace."[4] This love of Jesus is grace upon grace. It is greater than all our sin. Even when our sin increases, this grace abounds "all the more."[5]

It doesn't make sense, does it? Logic tells us that we deserve punishment for our transgressions—and perhaps even harsher punishment for those of us trapped in repetitive, addictive behaviors. It might seem wise to punish ourselves into sobriety; but as we've learned, punishment isn't love. Punishment can teach us an important lesson about real-life consequences, but it can't rehabilitate our souls; that's what grace is for.

3. Ephesians 3:19, NASB.

4. John 1:16, NASB.

5. Romans 5:20, NASB.

St. Paul wrote to the Colossians, "These are matters which have, to be sure, the appearance of wisdom in self-made religion and self-abasement and severe treatment of the body, but are of no value against fleshly indulgence."[6]

Rules, regulations, purity, and honor codes might make good common sense, but spiritual wisdom understands that man-made rules do not inspire the heart or fill the soul.

Only love can do that.

Who Will Do the Cleanup?

When I was a little girl, my family read a devotional pamphlet called *My Heart, Christ's Home*. It told us we needed to tidy up the "rooms" of our hearts so that they would be ready to welcome our holy Savior.

I was fascinated by this analogy. I wanted my heart to be a squeaky-clean vessel fit for Christ's presence. The problem was that I tried to clean it up all on my own. I felt all the obligations of holiness but also a great deal of fear, because I wasn't convinced God loved me unconditionally. Thus, my relationship with Jesus was one of timidity and foreboding.

Unfortunately, this way of thinking followed me into adulthood. I had a very strong sense of right and wrong, of moral obligation and duty. And I pushed myself to be pure, perfect, and worthy of having Jesus live inside my heart.

It wasn't until a few years ago when I was struggling to abstain from my addictive behaviors that I discovered something really important about the passage of Scripture where

6. Colossians 2:23, NASB.

St. Paul tells us in Ephesians 3:17 that Christ will live in our hearts. I'd always been so keen on getting to the Christ-inside-my-heart part that I overlooked the verse that came before: "I pray that from his glorious, unlimited resources he will empower you with inner strength through his Spirit."[7]

I was stunned: *God* will empower me? What would it be like, I wondered, to have God's unlimited resources aiding my spiritual sobriety? At the very least it would no longer be a death-match struggle!

But that's not all. Moving a little deeper into this passage, St. Paul promises that once Christ is dwelling in our hearts, "your roots will grow down into God's love and keep you strong."[8] This seemed like an impossible promise. I'd never felt rooted and grounded in God's love. I was taught that God's love was easily withheld if I misbehaved.

Could it be true what Paul says here? That our roots could grow deep into God's love, and that his love, not our own frantic effort, is the thing that will keep us strong?

The experience of addiction had caused me to believe that I was an inherently weak, horrible person. I didn't ask for God's help because I thought it was all on my shoulders to do the right thing. I thought it was my job to clean up the rooms of my heart. Why would God help me do what I alone was supposed to do?

And yet, here was St. Paul encouraging me that making my heart fit for Christ's presence was not something I had to accomplish on my own but rather something God enabled

7. Ephesians 3:16, NLT.
8. Ephesians 3:17, NLT.

me to do through His glorious, unlimited resources. What a relief!

Deep and Wide

Paul goes on to say,

> And may you have the power to understand, as all God's people should, how wide, how long, how high, and how deep this love is. May you experience the love of Christ, though it is too great to understand fully. Then you will be *made complete* with all the fullness of life and power that *comes from God.*[9]

This is what every religious addict needs, and it's what *everyone* needs: the power to understand and receive God's love. Because when we begin to understand the boundlessness of God's love for us, we can let our messy, addicted selves fall into it, knowing we are infinitely held and knowing that God is the one who will perform the work of recovery in our lives. If I could go back in time, I'd tell my little girl self that everything was going to be okay, that I didn't need to worry. "God's got this," I'd say. "God's got *you.*"

I'm not a little girl anymore. I'm all grown up and have kids of my own. Everything I know about God and spirituality I learned while changing thirty thousand diapers, breastfeeding five babies, and teaching toddlers that biting isn't an acceptable form of communication.

9. Ephesians 3:18–19, NLT; emphasis mine.

My theological training didn't exactly happen in a seminary, but I still learned the most important thing: some kind of vegetable with dinner is better than no vegetable at all (even if it's just a package of frozen mixed veggies heated up in the microwave)—which is to say, some kind of relationship with God is better than none at all. And when you're raising five kids, you can't afford fancy, so you make do with good enough. That's how I think of spiritual sobriety: not fancy, but good enough. And it *works*.

So, go ahead. Grab a forkful.

I won't tattle if you spit out the peas.

ACKNOWLEDGMENTS

THIS BOOK WOULDN'T HAVE BEEN POSSIBLE WITHOUT THE unflagging patience of my editors: Dave Kopp, Holly Halverson, and Derek Reed. Thanks for your sense of humor about my panicky, ALL-CAP E-MAILS. Thank you for letting me cry and argue and have panic attacks about this book—without letting me give up on it. Most of all, thank you for making my words sound way better and smarter than I am. Eternally grateful.

Thank you to my publisher, Convergent Books, for granting me the creative freedom I needed to develop, write, and *rewrite* this book. Which is to say, thank you for the deadline extensions. I'm humbled and honored.

Many thanks to my literary agent: Rachelle Gardner. Thank you for believing in me. You are the best cheerleader ever.

Much love to my blog readers, Facebook friends, and Twitter followers for reading my words and for having the ongoing conversation. Big, happy, fluffy hearts to all of you who so kindly contributed your stories and insights to these pages.

To my friends in the recovery community: Thank you for all your support. Thank you for taking my texts and phone calls, for listening to me, for providing wise feedback, and for encouraging me along the journey. Special love to Kim, Julia, Meg, Andie, Lauren, Tessa, Rob, Rachel, Bill, Nora, and Lora.

I'd also like to thank Fr. Al Baca for his wise counsel, prayers, and friendship. I am so grateful for the years you pastored at St. Cecilia's. Your gentle example of humility and compassion showed me how to be a Catholic Christian.

Lastly, all my love to my precious family: Matt, Jewel, James, Jude, Jorai & Jasiel. Y'all my peeps, yo.

RECOMMENDED READING
AND RESOURCES

Religious Addiction and/or Spiritual Abuse

Arterburn, Stephen, and Jack Felton. *Toxic Faith: Experiencing Healing from Painful Spiritual Abuse*. Colorado Springs, CO: Shaw, 2001.

Booth, Leo. *When God Becomes a Drug: Understanding Religious Addiction & Religious Abuse*. Los Angeles: J. P. Tarcher, 1991.

Esther, Elizabeth. *Girl at the End of the World: My Escape from Fundamentalism in Search of Faith with a Future*. New York: Convergent Books, 2014.

Johnson, David, and Jeffrey VanVonderen. *The Subtle Power of Spiritual Abuse*. Minneapolis, MN: Bethany House Publishers, 2005.

McFarland, Hillary, and Megan Lindsay. *Quivering Daughters: Hope and Healing for the Daughters of Patriarchy*. Austin, TX: DarkLight Publishing, 2010.

Minor, Robert N., PhD. *When Religion Is an Addiction*. St. Louis, MO: Humanity Works!, 2007.

Addiction and Relationships

Beattie, Melody. *Codependent No More: How to Stop Controlling Others and Start Caring for Yourself*. Center City, MN: Hazelden, 2011.

Carnes, Patrick. *A Gentle Path through the Twelve Steps*. Center City, MN: Hazelden, 2012.

Cloud, Henry, and John Townsend. *Boundaries: When to Say Yes, How to Say No to Take Control of Your Life*, rev. ed. Nashville, TN: Thomas Nelson, 1992.

Co-Dependents Anonymous, Inc. *Co-Dependents Anonymous*. Phoenix, AZ: CoDA Service Office, 1995.

Lalich, Janja, and Madeleine Tobias. *Take Back Your Life: Recovering from Cults and Abusive Relationships*. Berkeley, CA: Bay Tree Pub., 2006.

Mellody, Pia. *Facing Love Addiction: Giving Yourself the Power to Change the Way You Love*. New York: HarperOne, 2003.

Contemplative, Gentle Spirituality

Beattie, Melody. *The Language of Letting Go: Daily Meditations for Codependents*. Center City, MN: Hazelden, 1990.

Brown, C. Brené. *The Gifts of Imperfection: Let Go of Who You Think You're Supposed to Be and Embrace Who You Are*. Center City, MN: Hazelden, 2010.

Escobar, Kathy. *Faith Shift: Finding Your Way Forward When Everything You Believe Is Coming Apart*. New York: Convergent Books, 2014.

King, Heather. *Shirt of Flame: A Year with St. Thérèse of Lisieux*. Brewster, MA: Paraclete Press, 2011.

Linn, Dennis, Sheila Fabricant Linn, and Matthew Linn. *Good Goats: Healing Our Image of God*. Mahwah, NJ: Paulist Press, 1993.

Merton, Thomas, and Robert Inchausti. *Seeds*. Boston: Shambhala Publications, 2002.

Nouwen, Henri J. M. *The Inner Voice of Love: A Journey Through Anguish to Freedom*. New York: Doubleday, 1996.

Rohr, Richard. *Breathing Under Water: Spirituality and the Twelve Steps*. Cincinnati, OH: Franciscan Media, 2011.

Shapiro, Rami. *Recovery—The Sacred Art*. Woodstock, NY: Skylight Paths, 2009.

Singer, Michael A. *The Untethered Soul: The Journey Beyond Yourself.* Oakland, CA: New Harbinger Publications, 2007.

Online Resources

Co-Dependents Anonymous, www.coda.org

Godly Response to Abuse in the Christian Environment, www.netgrace .org

Homeschoolers Anonymous, www.homeschoolersanonymous.word press.com

Homeschool Alumni Reaching Out, www.hareachingout.wordpress .com

Sex and Love Addicts Anonymous, www.slaafws.org

Wellspring Retreat & Resource Center, www.wellspringretreat.org (assisting survivors of spiritual abuse)

1. How does the term *religious addiction* strike you? Do you think it's possible to become addicted to pious activity, church services, a spiritual leader? Have you known someone suffering from excessive devotion? Have you experienced it? What was the result?

2. How do you feel about the statement "The point of religion is not primarily that we feel better"? What is the goal of religion? When you have participated in spiritual services or rituals, what were you seeking? Did you get the result you sought? Did you ever pursue that result so ardently that you suffered negative consequences? Describe.

3. Which of the Common Beliefs and Behaviors of Sober Christians appeal to you most? Do you believe a healthy and satisfying relationship with God is possible for you? Why or why not?

4. How have you responded to emotionally charged services? Did you experience both the mountaintop high

and the valley of letdown? What did you do in response? Are these intense experiences where religious addiction started for you? Why or why not?

5. Can you identify any realities you've avoided in your pursuit of spiritual satisfaction? As you take steps toward sobriety, what will be hardest to face? Why?

6. What does the concept of *misericordia* mean to you? What compassionate strokes may God be enacting in your life? Do you see evidence of his loving pursuit of *you*? If so, how? If not, can you begin to look for his mercy at work in your life? How?

7. Does it make sense to you that frenzied activity and religious addiction spring from the same root—a need for God? Have any of your habits or behaviors become as compulsive as your pursuit of holiness? If so, which ones? What can you do to quell this different kind of addiction?

8. What kind of God have you served? When a religious addict, Elizabeth found him "wrathful and harsh," "stone silent" in answer to her prayers, hierarchal and inconsistent—sometimes he protected people from harm, sometimes he didn't. List some descriptors of your own. Do you believe this is the true nature of God, or do you hope for something better? Have you ever experienced him as Sandra did, as "completely loving," "infinitely boundless and compassionate"?

9. When have you most experienced Shame Brain? Was it while you were addictively serving God and never (in your own eyes) measuring up? Was it while you were enslaved to a different behavior that you could never seem

to stop? What can you now say in response to Shame Brain accusations?

10. Think about a time you engaged in a "verbal train wreck." Describe the situation. What did you do right? What didn't go so well? What does *sober* (or *kind*) *speech* mean to you? How could you have used that tool during your "train wreck"?

11. What do you think of Nadia Bolz-Weber's assertion, "The sacred rest that is yours never comes from being worthy"? In what ways can you make rest from the pursuit of worthiness part of your search for sobriety?

12. Describe the power of setting and upholding boundaries. Have you seen some in use? Have you ever tried to put this tool to work? What happened? What steps are most important for creating appropriately tough boundaries?

13. As you embrace spiritual sobriety, do you anticipate staying with your current church, changing to a new one, or putting church aside, at least for now? Why? Describe your ideal church—making allowances for the human imperfection that will always be present.

14. How hard have you tried to be *good*? What was the result? How would emphasizing honesty instead change your life and habits? List the benefits.

15. Describe what relapse would look like (or has looked like) for you. Do you define relapse as failure—or just a speed bump on the road to sobriety? How can relapse actually help you commit more fully to your spiritual health?

ABOUT THE AUTHOR

ELIZABETH ESTHER is the author of *Girl at the End of the World: My Escape from Fundamentalism in Search of Faith with a Future*. She lives in Southern California with her husband and five children. You can find her online at elizabethesther.com.